The

# PSYCHOLOGICAL ASPECTS
of the
# AGING PROCESS

The

# PSYCHOLOGICAL ASPECTS

of the

# AGING PROCESS

With Sociological Implications

*By*

**HAROLD GEIST, Ph.D.**

*Lecturer in Psychology*
*San Francisco State University*
*San Francisco, California*
*Staff, Everett Gladman*
*Memorial Hospital*
*Oakland, California*

ROBERT E. KRIEGER PUBLISHING COMPANY
HUNTINGTON, NEW YORK
1981

Original edition 1968
Second edition 1981


Printed and Published by
**ROBERT E. KRIEGER PUBLISHING CO., INC.**
**645 New York Avenue**
**Huntington, New York 11743**

Copyright © 1968 (original material) by Warren H. Green, Inc.
Transferred to Harold Geist 1972
Copyright © 1980 (new material) by
Robert E. Krieger Publishing Co., Inc.

Printed in the United States of America

**Library of Congress Cataloging in Publication Data**

Geist, Harold.
   The Psychological aspects of the aging process with
sociological implications.

   Includes bibliographies and index.
   1.   Old age.   2.   Aging—Psychological aspects.
3.   Aging—Social aspects.   I.   Title.
BF724.8.G4      1980         155.67         80-13233
ISBN 0-89874-073-8

# FOREWORD

Wᴵᴛʜ ᴛʜᴇ ᴛʀᴇᴍᴇɴᴅᴏᴜsʟʏ rapid increase of the aged in this and other countries, I thought it necessary to give an overview of the entire aging process in simple terms which could be used by students, laymen and professional people in the field. Many treatises on aging are so complicated that they are useless except as reference books to be stored away in libraries for future use on specific topics. The science of gerontology is now divided into many areas, but the psychological and sociological aspects are indispensably fused. Contemporary psychological research with the aged has far-reaching sociological implications, not only insofar as older people are concerned, but also the young and middle aged are affected. The rapid growth of segregated communities of the aged has given rise to new problems, problems which can only be solved if one knows the psychology of the aged as individuals and in groups. Thus, in this book both the psychology and psychopathology of older people are discussed initially, and the sociological implications are explained in terms of group behavior in later chapters. Culture has an important bearing on how the aged are treated, and thus I thought it important to discuss the whole problem of aging in many countries other than the United States. The implications of aging in the Scandinavian countries, England, Germany, Holland, Switzerland, Luxembourg, Rumania, South America, Canada, Israel, Japan and the Soviet Union gives balanced perspective to what is being done in the United States.

My thanks go to the staff of Napa State Hospital, California, particularly the late Doctor Gordon Riley, former Chief of the

v

Psychology Department, and to Doctors Ramona Todd and the late Wrenshall Oliver from whom I learned much on the geriatric service. I would also like to thank Mrs. Florence White who painstakingly typed the manuscript and Warren Green, former publisher, for his encouragement.

HAROLD GEIST
*Berkeley, California*

# TABLE OF CONTENTS

The
# PSYCHOLOGICAL ASPECTS
of the
# AGING PROCESS

*Chapter I*

[handwritten: Milieu— an environment, medium, or condition; background, sphere) surroundings, element.]

# INTRODUCTION

## IMPORTANCE OF THE STUDY OF THE AGING PROCESS

THE NUMERICAL increase in the population of the elderly is proceeding at a fantastic rate. The total population of the United States increased about 7% from 1956 to 1966, while the number of persons 65 and over increased 35% in the same interval. 4,000 people enter into the 65 age level every day and only 1,000 die leaving an excess of 1,000 everyday. There were about 19 million people in the United States in 1966 over the age of 65. In 1975 there were 22 million and it's projected in the year 2,000 11.1% of the population will be age 65 and over. Because of this large number of aged people, it behooves society to create a milieu in which this large group of people get maximum satisfaction and happiness and in which advice is available about various retirement questions and, in addition, the aspects of aging are studied in a scientific way which will enable the older segments of the population to live more fruitful and creative lives. In spite of the fact that aging is primarily a wearing out process, some people seem to gain momentum as they mature. Titian painted his finest pictures just before he died in his hundredth year; Goethe worked until he was past 80, his intellect unimpaired, and wrote some of his finest poems when he passed his 75th birthday. William Cullen Bryant wrote until his death at 89 and Gladstone became famous after the age of 60 and was elected Prime Minister four times, still retaining the office at 82. Thomas Edison, at the age of 70, during the first World War, designed, built, and operated several benzol plants and was made Chairman of the Naval Advisory Board. Women who have made their mark in advancing years are numerous. The mother of the famous physician, Sir

3

William Osler, was a woman of great energy and character, and died at a very advanced age. Clara Barton, head of the Red Cross, accomplished much in her advancing years; Elizabeth Blackwell, who together with her sister Emily founded the Women's Medical College, did most of her useful work at an advanced age. Grandma Moses is a prime example of a woman who was at the height of her creative powers at an advanced age. Other people who were creative, productive, and happy at an advanced age include John D. Rockefeller, Winston Churchill, Oliver Wendell Holmes, Thomas Masaryk, Charles DeGaulle, and many others. In any consideration of the process of aging, the term "successful aging" must be considered. Havighurst (1) says that successful aging has two principal implications. One is high self regard and a display of contentment with life, and secondly, a regard by his peers, i.e., does the individual fulfill his social role and interpersonal obligations. These two criteria, inner and outer, are not always concomitant, but most of the people mentioned above have met these criteria of successful aging. With so many more people living to an advanced age, successful aging is becoming ever more important in an older society.

## NATURE OF THE AGING PROCESS

The scientific study of aging, known as gerontology, is primarily concerned with the time between maturity and death. In analyzing various factors which influence this period of life, Shock (2) divides the problem of gerontology into four major categories:

1. The social and economic problems caused by an increasing number of elderly people in the population.
2. The psychological aspects of aging along with their reaction to one another.
3. The physiological bases of aging along with pathological deviations and disease processes.
4. The general biological aspects of aging in all animal species.

*Social and economic problems.* War, famine, and pestilence have caused severe shifts in population structure. However, these destructive forces have been balanced by the constructive ones of increased medical knowledge and the lessened hardships of modern civilization, enabling many less vigorous youth to survive into full maturity and even old age. The need of the aging for economic and health security is being met by governmental legislation such as Social Security and Medicare. One of the major issues in the whole range of social and economic problems of the aged is that of employment. The problems of continued employment of older workers, the augmentation of productivity of the older employed, the age of retirement of workers, and leisure in senescence, will increase as time goes by because of the increasing life span. The kinds of employment that the aged will seek will depend in part upon such psychological considerations as the motivation, learning capacity, and retraining potential of the elderly person.

*Psychological Aspects.* The psychological aspects of aging involve a wide variety of problems. The effect of aging on certain needs and motives, the effect of prior experience in the aging process, the psychodynamics of the emotional life of the elderly, the effect of age upon learning, the effect of age on psychomotor performance, and the role and importance of sensory changes in aging, are particularly important. Psychopathology and aging and the problem of the adjustment of the individual to the aging process with tangential considerations of the changing opportunities, expectations, or limitations upon adjustment set by the culture are important psychological aspects of aging. Changing adjustment may in turn be a causal condition determined by a variety of personality and other changes with age and also encompasses the gamut of the psychological aspects of the aging process. The emotional needs of the elderly have been studied intensively by a variety of experts in different disciplines, but physiological and medical research are integral parts of this element.

*Physiology and Disease.* The disease characteristics of the senescent period differ widely from those common in youth. With advancing years, there occurs a sharp rise in the incidence of the so-called degenerative disorders. The major diseases whose incidence reflects the effect of aging include cardiovascular diseases, diabetes mellitus, gout, cancer, disorders of the climacterium and various arthritic diseases whose etiology is primarily insidious and endogenous and both chronic and persistently progressive as opposed to the disorders of youth which are infectious, communicable, acute, and have an exogenous etiology.

*Biological Aspects of Aging.* The biology of aging is primarily concerned with explaining why organisms tend to live certain lengths of life. Time is the principal element of the biology of the aging process. With the passage of time, certain things happen to species, organs, cells, and the organism as a whole. There are inevitable time dependent processes that limit the capacity of the older organisms and cells to sustain themselves. These processes give rise to concepts known as "biological clocks" in which during the passage of time certain substances are dissipated and damage to the organism occurs. For example, cellular death, a characteristic of aging, is now considered to be caused by the damage to the genetic material of the cell. Chemically, this is called desoxyribonucleic acid (DNA) which leads to the formation of ribonucleic acid (RNA) which synthesizes the enzymes necessary for cellular function. If the enzymes are not present or are defective, the cell cannot survive. It has been speculated that somewhere within the chromosomes there are sites which are particularly susceptible to damage with the passage of time. It has also been shown that cells that do not or cannot divide seem to show aging more than cells that do divide. In man, certain important cells do not divide: e.g., neurones of the nervous system and muscle cells. It appears that these cells are critical in the potential for long life. The biological potential for aging is not only limited by genetic endowment but also by environment and disease processes. In general, aging produces the following kinds of organic changes:

1. An increase in connective tissue in the organism.
2. A gradual loss of elastic properties of connective tissue.
3. A dissappearance of cellular elements in the nervous system.
4. A reduction in the number of normally functioning cells.
5. An increased amount of fat.

6. A decrease in oxygen utilization.
7. A decrease in the amount of blood pumped by the heart under resting conditions.
8. A lesser amount of air expired by the lungs than in a younger organism.
9. Decreased muscular strength.
10. The excretion of hormones especially by the sex glands and the adrenal glands is lower than normal.

## HISTORY OF THE PSYCHOLOGY OF AGING

The study of the psychology of the aging process began with the publication of a book in 1835 by a Belgian by the name of Quetelet entitled *Sur l'Homme et le Developpement de ses Facultes.* Quetelet was an accomplished man and was versed in mathematics, statistics, astronomy, and psychology. Researchers representing various disciplines have made profound observations on psychological differences of people of different ages. Shakespeare, for example, had his *Seven Ages of Man* mounted in stained glass windows above his tomb in the Collegiate Church of the Holy Trinity in Stratford-on-Avon in England. Galton may be considered the second man who engaged in the purposeful fathering of measurements in the psychology of aging almost simultaneously with the founding, in 1879, by Wundt of the psychological laboratory at Leipzig. The primary contribution of Galton to the study of aging is the data gathered by his Anthropometric Laboratory at the International Health Exhibition in London in 1884. At that time, over 9000 males and females age 5-80 were measured in 17 different ways.

The objective study of the psychology of aging began in the 19th Century. In various countries, particularly in Europe, physiologists and physicians began to make observations about aging. In Russia, Pavlov made many contributions to the aging process by correlating psychological and physiological processes. During this period, there also was a good deal of descriptive work in the manner in which man's senses and faculties develop and change with advancing age. At this time, these descriptions were based not on intuition but on measurements and quantitative statistical methods. After World War I, G. S. Hall, in his book *Senescence,* published in 1922, began the systemetic study of the development of the aging process. He turned from a specialization of child psychology to that of the aging process and began a series of interesting departures from contemporary opinion concerning aging and religious belief and fear of death. It has been commonly believed (and is today by many people) that old people approaching death would be more fearful and hence become more religious to reconcile themselves to an uncertain future. Hall believed that old people do not necessarily show an increase in religious interest nor are they more fearful of the idea of death but rather that the fear of death is a young man's concern. His ideas here touched on the whole problem central to personality theory regarding fear and anxiety reduction and cognitive theory. The first major research unit devoted to the psychology of aging was established by Miles in 1928 at Stanford University. There was an aborted attempt to do experimental work with "mature" people in the San Francisco, California, Bay Area with headquarters at Stanford. Miles gave his presidential address before the American Psychological Association in 1932 based on the results of the Stanford Later Maturity Project. His chapter in the first edition (1939) of *Cowdry's Problem of Aging* showed that the psychology of aging has become an appreciable area of knowledge, comparing very favorably with contributions from other disciplines and sciences.

As the result of the work of Bühler and Frenkel-Brunswick, the whole man was studied and age changes in values and progression of individuals toward their life goals as revealed by biographical studies were scrutinized. Later, E. K. Strong in his monumental studies on interest measurement broadened the scope of the psychology of aging with his studies of changes of interests with age. It was during the 1930's with the publication of *Cowdry's Problems of Aging* that psychologists first began to see the desirability of considering aging as a comprehensive subject and that aging should also include related disciplines such as physiology. Later that same year, Birren negotiated with the Surgeon General of the U. S. Public Health Service for the

establishment of a section on aging. Initially, this had been subsidized by the Macy Foundation but was later absorbed in the
federal budget. Stieglitz became the first director of this section
and also at that time acted as Secretary for the National Advisory
Committee on Gerontology. The United States Public Health
Service made funds available for many research projects on aging.
After a year, Nathan Shock took the place of Stieglitz, and Shock
later became Chief of the Gerontology Branch of the National
Heart Institute and the Baltimore City Hospitals and is one of
the most astute experts and investigators in the entire field of
aging. After World War II, there was increased expansion in the
field of gerontology with new laboratories and research centers
mushrooming in this country. In 1945, a group headed by Pressey
organized a Division of Maturity and Old Age of the American
Psychological Association.

In 1953, the Section on Aging as part of the National Institute
of Mental Health was organized with Birren as its head. In 1974
Congress authorized the formation of the National Institute on
Aging in Washington, D.C. The formation of the International
Association of Gerontology, and its first meeting in Liege, gave
the first major opportunity for psychologists and people from
other disciplines to exchange information on an international
level. The United States has been most active in research in this
area. Some of the most prominent contributions to social
psychological research have been those of Havighurst and his
group of the Committee on Human Development at the
University of Chicago. Certain key names are prominent in the
psychological literature. These are Harold Jones, John Anderson,
Irving Lorge, Birren, and others. Currently, there are few Western
countries which do not have one psychologist or related scientist
concerned with aging. The most outstanding are Bourliere, of the
Centre de Gerontologil Claude Bernard in Paris, Verzar, a
physiologist at the Institut für Experimentalle Gerontologie in
Basel, and Heron, the Director of the Unit for Research on
Occupational Aspects of Aging at the University of Liverpool
under the auspices of Great Britain's Medical Research Council.

## Demographic Considerations

### THE AGED IN THE POPULATION AS A WHOLE

As noted earlier, the proportion of older people in the population of the United States and throughout the world is increasing at a very rapid rate. Between 1900 and 1950, the total population of the United States doubled but the number of people 65 and older quadrupled. Census extrapolations indicated that in 1975 there were about 20.7 million over the age of 65. In all probability, the estimates will be low since past experience of the Bureau of the Census is that predictions of future populations are usually underestimated rather than overestimated.

Thus, a man 50 years old today has a 74% chance to survive to the normal retirement age of 65. Having lived until he reaches 65, he has better than an even chance to live to age 75. It is estimated that one cut of eight survive to the 85th year and in the year 2000, in the United States, one out of four will survive to the 85th year. Figure 1 shows life expectancy from early times to the present in various cultures. The increment from Roman and Grecian times to the last half century is indeed striking.

TABLE 1
AVERAGE LIFE EXPECTANCY FOR SELECTED AGE GROUPS

| At Age | Years Remaining for Men | For Women |
|--------|-------------------------|-----------|
| 35 | 35.4 | 39.9 |
| 40 | 30.9 | 35.3 |
| 45 | 26.5 | 30.5 |
| 50 | 22.4 | 26.2 |
| 55 | 18.8 | 22.0 |
| 60 | 15.4 | 18.1 |
| 65 | 12.4 | 14.4 |
| 70 | 9.8 | 11.2 |
| 75 | 7.5 | 8.3 |
| 80 | 5.4 | 5.8 |
| 85 | 3.6 | 3.7 |

In 1965, the Bureau of the Census figures show that the 65 and older group now number 18 million and there are almost 19 million retired people today who represent 10% of the population. Half of the elderly are more than 73 years old; the median age level has been increasing gradually each year since 1950 when it was 72 years.

Figure 1 indicates that the average age of death has been increasing steadily in the United States from 35 years in 1879 to 67.5 years in 1955 for white males. It is estimated that within the next 10 years it will be over 75 years for males and 80 for females.

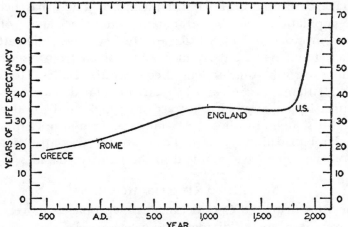

Figure 1. Life expectancy from early times to the present, A.D. 500-1950 (estimated average age at death). Data from L. I. Dublin, A. J. Lotka, and M. Spiegelman, *Length of Life* (rev. ed., New York, Ronald Press, 1949), p. 42.

The increase in life expectancy in this country is not restricted to any socio-economic group, race, or color; all classes of the population, white and Negro, male and female, rich and poor, have taken part in this gain.

## REGIONAL DIFFERENCES

There are also regional differences. In New England, the aged constitute a larger proportion of the total population than elsewhere. In Maine, New Hampshire, Vermont, and Massachusetts, the proportion is greater than the nation as a whole. Four states in the farm belt — Iowa, Kansas, Missouri, and Nebraska — and one mountain state, Montana, also have a relatively high proportion of aged persons as a result of emigration of the younger generation. The proportion of the aged in the population of California and Florida, which is still below the national average, is attributed to immigration of older people, most of them retired.

## MIGRATION OF THE ELDERLY

Between 1940 and 1950, the greatest change in the proportion of persons over 65 occurred in Arizona. California, and Nevada. Although these states gained substantially in total population, the percentage of people over 65 still increased. There has been a shift of population from the rural areas to the cities and $\frac{4}{5}$ of the aged live in cities and towns. Relatively few *large* cities attract significant numbers of elderly men and women from elsewhere. Exceptions are Los Angeles, San Diego, Seattle, Dallas, Houston, Memphis, Atlanta, Miami, and Jacksonville, Florida. State capitals and university towns seem to attract old people and to offer the type of life sought by those who migrate. Southern California, Peninsular Florida, and eastern Texas are the principal areas to which older people have migrated in the past two decades.

## MOVERS AND NON-MOVERS

The Bureau of the Census categorizes people as movers and non-movers. Movers are divided into a few groups, those moving to a different house in the same county, a different county in the state, a different state, and abroad. As indicated in Tables 2 and

TABLE 2
PERCENTAGE OF MOVERS AND NON-MOVERS, TOTAL[a]
AND AGED POPULATION, UNITED STATES, 1955-1960.
% DISTRIBUTION

| Age | Total | Non-movers (%) | Same County | Movers Different County Same State | Different State | Other[b] |
|---|---|---|---|---|---|---|
| Total population | | | | | | |
| 5 years and over | 100 | 50 | 30 | 9 | 9 | 2 |
| 65 years and over | 100 | 64 | 18 | 12 | 4 | 2 |
| 65-69 | 100 | 70 | 20 | 4 | 4 | 2 |
| 70-74 | 100 | 71 | 19 | 4 | 4 | 2 |
| 75 & over | 100 | 54 | 16 | 25 | 3 | 2 |

Source of Data: Tables 1 and 3. U. S. Bureau of the Census (1960[a]).

[a]"Total population" refers to persons five years of age and older in 1960. Children born during the period 1955-1960 are excluded in order that the population base consists only of persons who could have moved during the entire five-year period.

[b]"Other" includes persons living abroad in 1960 and those who moved but whose 1955 residence was not reported.

3, older people were less mobile than the total population during 1955-1960; 64% remained in the same house compared with 50% of the total population. Only 4% of older people moved to another state while 9% of the total population made one or more interstate moves. Mobility patterns also remain constant from ages 65-74. After age 75, mobility increases reflecting changes associated with retirement, widowhood and institutionalization. As with the older segment of the population, the younger and middle aged people who have moved did so within the bounds of their own state. Mobility seems to decline with age but the decline is gradual and movement is at a relatively low level throughout much of middle as well as old age.

TABLE 3

PERCENTAGE OF TOTAL AND AGED POPULATION MAKING INTRA-STATE AND INTERSTATE MOVES, UNITED STATES, 1935-1940, 1955-1960.

| Age | % Intrastate Movers | | % Interstate Movers | |
|---|---|---|---|---|
| | 1935-1940 | 1955-1960 | 1935-1940 | 1955-1960 |
| Total population | | | | |
| 5 years and over | 8 | 9 | 5 | 9 |
| 65 years & over | 4 | 12 | 3 | 4 |

Source of data: Shryock, 1964, Table 11, 18, page 362, and Table above.

PERCENTAGE OF INTERSTATE MOVERS BY AGE
UNITED STATES, 1955-1960.

| Age | % Interstate Movers | Age | % Interstate Movers |
|---|---|---|---|
| 5-9 | 10.0 | 45-49 | 5.5 |
| 10-14 | 7.5 | 50-54 | 4.7 |
| 15-19 | 9.9 | 55-59 | 4.2 |
| 20-24 | 19.8 | 60-64 | 4.1 |
| 25-29 | 17.9 | 65-69 | 4.5 |
| 30-34 | 12.2 | 70-75 | 4.0 |
| 35-39 | 9.5 | 75+ | 3.5 |
| 40-44 | 7.2 | Total population 5 years and over | 9.0 |

Source of Data: Table 2, U. S. Bureau of the Census (1960a).

It is interesting to note the socio-economic and educational characteristics associated with greater and lesser movement of older people.

*Education.* There seems to be no relationship between education and mobility for aged persons of either sex. Approximately

70% of older men and women at each educational level (grade school, high school, college) were living in the same house in 1955-1960.

*Employment Status.* As would be expected, employed older men and women are the least mobile followed by the retired who in turn are less mobile than the unemployed.

*Income.* The statistics* on median income for various family categories (all families, husband-wife families, other families with male heads and those with females as head of the family) show that aged non-movers had higher incomes than movers in all family categories.

*Marital Status.* Separated and divorced aged men and women were the most mobile of all status categories. Forty-nine per cent of such men and 41% of the women changed residences at least once between 1955 and 1960. Married men and women are the least mobile. Single and widowed people have identical mobility patterns falling between that of the married and separated and divorced.

*Reasons for Moving.* Why do the aged move? An investigation carried out by the Survey Research Center at the University of Michigan in 1962-1963 indicated that with advancing age, the proportion of movers who cited job transfers, education to help prepare for work, or other economic reasons for moving, declined steadily. Over 80% of movers aged 18-24 cite economic reasons for moving while only 20% of those over 65 do so. Family and community reasons are important in moving for those over 65. Thus, mobility for the aged depends essentially on climate, special housing, or care facilities, an opportunity to be near or live with relatives, or possibly lower cost of living. In some states, favorable tax provisions and liberal welfare programs attract the aged. It is expected that in time the aged can be expected to exhibit higher rates of mobility and this geographical mobility may become of great importance to the older segment and those who study them.

---

*U. S. Census, 1960.

## BIBLIOGRAPHY

1. Havighurst, Robert, and Albrecht, Ruth: *Older People.* New York. David McCay Company, 1953.
2. Shock, Nathan: *Trends in Gerontology.* Stanford, Stanford University Press, 1957.

## General References

1. Birren, J. E.: *Handbook of Aging in the Individual.* Chicago, Univ. of Chicago Press, 1959.
2. Burgess, E. W. (ed.) : *Aging in Western Societies.* Chicago, Univ. Chicago Press, 1960.
3. Burstein, Sona R.: Papers in the historical background of gerontology. *Geriatrics, 10:*189-193, 328-332, 536-540, 1955.
4. Cowdry, E. V. (ed.) : *Problems of Aging,* 2nd Ed. Baltimore, Williams and Wilkins, 1942, pp. 810-31.
5. Hall, G. S.: *Senescence.* New York, Appleton-Century Crofts, 1922.
6. Laslett, P., Harrison, J., Clayworth, and Cogenhoe: In Bell, H. E., and Ollard, R. L. (eds) : *Historical Essays 1600-1750.* pp. 157-184, London, Adam and Charles Black, Ltd., 1963.
7. Quetelet, A.: *Sur l'homme et le developpement de ses facultés.* Paris, Bachelier, Imprimeur Libraire, 2 vols., 1835.
8. Simmons, L. W.: *The Role of the Aged in Primitive Society.* New Haven, Yale University Press, 1945.

# Chapter II

# PERSONALITY THEORY AND THE AGING PROCESS

THERE IS A dearth of conceptualization of the aging process in contemporary theories of personality. Actually, the discussion of aging by the Chinese and Hindu philosophers and the thinkers of Western culture such as Nietszche and Schopenhauer is more copious than that of the personality theoreticians. Philosophers thought that since death is certain, real happiness depends upon the capabilities of old people to overcome their own selfishness in the interest of other people's welfare and happiness. "Only he who gives himself completely without regard for his own person will at the end be free from anxiety and deep concern when the last hour is approaching and remain free and unhampered from emotional crisis in old age." However, let us consider some of the extant theories which have been related to the aging process, which at best are only superficially related to aging.

## CONSTITUTION THEORY AND AGING

Kretschmer developed a typology by relating the two major types of mental disorder, manic-depressive psychosis and schizophrenia, to certain patterns in physique, the leptosomic and pyknic types. Kretschmer added two additional types, the athletic and dysplastic. He suggested that psychotic states are directly continuous with normal behavior and that there are intermediary states tending toward abnormality which he calls cycloid and schizoid.

Following the lead of Kretschmer, Sheldon gathered data on the physique of several thousand people age 18-63 and presented age curves differing markedly as to their peak, form, and the rate of increase and decrease between the various somatotype families.*

Sheldon theorized that when a particular somatotype is stationary or is ascending in size in middle age and later in the 60's, it indicates this will be an enduring somatotype. Differences in personalities between younger and older men can be explained by the endurance of a specific somatotype. He maintained that it is not the somatotype itself which decreases life or the specific organ weakness associated with it. The followers of Kretschmer such as Schmering and Conrad conceived constitution as a biogenetic problem. They conceived the different constitutional types as developmental stages through which a person passes in the course of his life. As he grows older, an individual tends more toward the leptosomic physique. The studies of Ufland and Boehmig represent more recent research on the influence of constitution and age which must await experimental verification.

## PSYCHOANALYSIS AND AGING

In one of Freud's earlier papers (1), he discusses the appreciation of psychoanalytic techniques as a therapeutic measure, and says "Near and above the fifties the elasticity of the mental process on which the treatment depends is lacking. Old people are no longer educable and on the other hand the mass of material to be dealt with would prolong the duration of the treatment indefinitely." In 1898, Freud stated that "psychoanalysis loses its effectiveness after the patient is too advanced in years." Freud has made comments on the "elasticity of the ego" in older people. This "ego rigidity" results in fixed opinions and reactions. In addition to the more objective evaluation of reality factors as people get older, there is an increase in awareness of childhood conflicts. Abraham modified this position and demonstrated that psychoanalytic therapy *was* applicable for older people. Jelliffe and his co-workers tried psychoanalytic therapy with older people and stated that psychoanalysis, slightly modified, was applicable

---

*Very briefly these are viscerotonia, somatotonia, and cerebrotonia as the three primary components of human personality, the first and third similar to Kretschmer's cycloid and schizoid temperments, the second in-between.

partly as a therapeutic method and definitely as a research instrument. Kaufman, a psychoanalyst, states that the psychoses and neuroses of this period are definitely of a pregenital type. In discussing the analytic treatment of depressions of old age, he refers to the "inverted Oedipus complex" where aged and dependent individuals regard adult offspring as they formerly regarded their own parents. There is considerable ambivalence when an older person who once guided his children in growth now has to be responsible to them.

Helene Deutsch has studied the effect of old age in women. The functions of reproduction and the loss of direct object relationships are the chief centers of conflict in the older woman. The menopause and climacterium is a psychologically traumatic experience to every woman and represents a narcissistic injury. With the onset of this period going along with a regression in physiological functioning, there is a heightening of life activity and a displaced reaching out for new love objects. There is a retrogression to abandoned earlier drives. The kinds of psychotic manifestations during this period of life are an indication of the many conflict situations which have arisen. For example, the agitated and involutional depressions, and paranoid conditions are indicative of the regression which has taken place.

Grotjahn, who is reported to treat geriatric patients successfully with psychoanalysis, believes that growing old represents a narcissistic trauma since it represents and repeats a castration threat. The neuroses of old age are defenses against castration anxiety.

Some analysts have extended the Freudian theory and therapeutic method directly to geriatrics and gerontology. Hamilton, for example, distinguishes four turning points in the human life cycle: 1) Termination of infancy; 2) Termination of childhood and beginning of adolescence; 3) Transition from adolescence to maturity; and 4) The period of change from mature to aging personality. According to Hamilton, the latter period is characterized as a regression to the first two stages of development. In the beginning of senescence, there is a weakening of unconscious urges. Probably much of this decrease is socially conditioned and brought about by retirement and leads to inactivity requiring new orientation and adjustment. The great demands made by the ego, unable to cope with the instinctual urges of the id, result in feelings of inferiority, insecurity, and guilt as well as concomitant feelings of aggression and hostility toward younger people. The pre-existing and chronically unresolved conflicts of infancy and childhood, repressed during later maturity become reactivated under old age and lead to infantile and neurotic behavior.

Neurotic aggression which may be intrinsically a sexual problem is dramatized by the number of aging men experiencing sexual impulses which take a socially and biologically forbidden direction and which often lead to accusations of exhibitionism, aggressive sexual offenses against young girls, or homosexual assaults against boys. Autoerotic genital behavior of older men, the growing preoccupation with bodily sensations, hypochondriacal disturbances, and increased urination which is evidence of prostatic problems, further substantiate these regressive tendencies. Complete proof must await further experimental investigation.

**Erikson's Epigenetic Theory**

Hartman elaborated on Freud's theory of ego development, including a general theory of reality relations in which he stressed the special role of social relations. However, it remained for Erikson in his epigenetic theory, which centers on the ego, to complete the elaboration of the role of social reality and outline a sequence of phases of personality in terms of psychosocial development. This sequence of phases parallels and goes beyond that of Freud's theory of libido development. Thus, Erikson was the first in the history of psychoanalytic theory to encompass those phases of the life cycle which we usually find under the single concept of genital maturity. Erikson describes each phase in terms of successful and unsuccessful solutions which can be arrived at, though in reality the outcome is a balance between these extremes. Erikson divides the life cycle into phase-specific developmental tasks which must be solved. These are: 1) Basic trust vs. mistrust. 2) Autonomy vs. shame and doubt. 3) Initiative vs. guilt. 4) Industry vs. inferiority. 5) Identity vs. identity diffusion. 6) Intimacy vs. isolation. 7) Geniality vs. despair.

He postulates a "cogwheeling" of the life cycles. The representatives of society or "caretaking people" are coordinated to the developing individual by their inborn responsiveness to his needs and by what Erikson calls "phase-specific needs of their own." The "caretaking people" are representatives of their society as carriers of traditional institutional caretaking patterns. The theory focuses on the fact that each society meets each phase of the development of its members by institutions (parental care, schools, teachers, occupations, etc.) specific to it and insures that the developing individual will be viable in it.

The distinctive pattern of Erikson's theory is that it offers a conceptual explanation of the individual's social development by observing the unfolding of the genetically social character of the human individual in the course of his encounter with the social environment. The theory becomes directly related in a developmental way to the dynamic problems of old age. Erikson's theory ranges over the phenomenological — specifically: clinical psychoanalytic and general psychoanalytic psychosocial propositions. In discussing the problem of identity formation, Erikson describes an "evolving configuration" — a configuration which is gradually established by successive ego syntheses and resyntheses through childhood. He brings the whole concept to fruition in a diagram which envisages the epigenetic principle of childhood as a gradual unfolding of the personality through phase-specific crises.

This diagram (Fig. 2) shows the sequence of psychosocial crises and development of the component parts of the psychosocial personality. It can be seen that the 8th vertical contains "integrity vs. despair" which is characteristic of mature age. Erikson does not define what he means by integrity but he provides several attributes. "It is the acceptance of one's own and only life cycle and of the people who have become significant to it as something that had to be and that by necessity permitted of no substitutions. It thus means a new and different love of one's parents, free of the wish that they would have been different and the acceptance of one's life as one's own responsibilities. . . . Although

| | 1. | 2. | 3. | 4. | 5. | 6. | 7. | 8. |
|---|---|---|---|---|---|---|---|---|
| I. INFANCY | Trust vs. Mistrust | | | | Unipolarity vs. Premature Self-Differentation | | | |
| II. EARLY CHILDHOOD | | Autonomy vs. Shame, Doubt | | | Bipolarity vs. Autism | | | |
| III. PLAY AGE | | | Initiative vs. Guilt | | Play Identification vs. (oedipal) Fantasy Identities | | | |
| IV. SCHOOL AGE | | | | Industry vs. Inferiority | Work Identification vs. Identity Foreclosure | | | |
| V. ADOLESCENCE | Time Perspective vs. Time Diffusion | Self-Certainty vs. Identity Consciousness | Role Experimentation vs. Negative Identity | Anticipation of Achievement vs. Work Paralysis | Identity vs. Identity Diffusion | Sexual Identity vs. Bisexual Diffusion | Leadership Polarization vs. Authority Diffusion | Ideological Polarization vs. Diffusion of Ideals |
| VI. YOUNG ADULT | | | | | Solidarity vs. Social Isolation | Intimacy vs. Isolation | | |
| VII. ADULTHOOD | | | | | | | Generativity vs. Self-Absorption | |
| VIII. MATURE AGE | | | | | | | | Integrity vs. Disgust, Despair |

Figure 2.

aware of the relationship of all the various life styles which have given meaning to human striving, the possessor of integrity is ready to defend the dignity of his own life style against all the physical and economic threats. . . .

"The loss of this accrued ego integration is signified by despair and an often unconscious fear of death. The one and only life cycle is not accepted as the ultimate of life. Despair expresses the feeling that the time is short, too short for the attempt to start another life and try out alternative roads to integrity. Such a despair is often hidden behind a show of disgust, a misanthropy, or a chronic contemptuous displeasure with particular institutions and particular people — a disgust and displeasure which (where not allied with constructive ideas and a life cooperation) only signify the individual's contempt of himself" (2). One can readily see the adaptation of the elderly to their psychosocial environment in terms of Erikson's theory.

Charlotte Bühler was one of the first to undertake empirical studies to determine what general principles hold for change over the lifespan and the kinds of needs in various phases of adulthood. Other theorists such as Fromm and Maslow have made important clinical contributions to the study of adult personality but have not formulated any systematic theories regarding each personality.

## INDIVIDUAL PSYCHOLOGY THEORY

Adler has made allusions to later life in discussing his theory of individual psychology. Old age is characterized by strong inferiority feelings and is deeply rooted in the patient's past. This is often caused by intellectual and physical insufficiency and external events such as financial loss, the breaking away from the responsibilities of work on retirement, and the dissolution of the family. Ansbacher and Ansbacher, who recently systematized Adler's theories, state that aging people in our society are severely threatened because old age affects them like other disparagents of self esteem.

## JUNGIAN PSYCHOLOGY AND THE AGING PROCESS

Jung, differing with Freud, organized human life into three chronological stages. The first stage, up to about the third or fourth year, he calls the pre-sexual stage. There he sees the libido or life energy occupied chiefly with nutrition and growth. The second stage includes the years from the fourth year to puberty and he speaks of this period as the prepubertal. The third stage is that from puberty onward and can be considered the time of maturity. One of Jung's concepts that stands in direct contradiction to those of Freud, which bears directly on the aging process, is the refusal to see in the infantile past the cause of the later development of illness. Jung places the cause of pathogenic conflicts *at the present moment* and considers that in seeking the cause in the distant past one is following the patient's desire to withdraw himself as much as possible from the present.

The conflict, Jung continues, is produced by some important task or duty which is biologically essential and practical for the fulfillment of the individual's ego; as an obstacle arises he shrinks and stops and thus halted, cannot go on. With this interference in the path of progression, libido is stored and a regression takes place which causes an reanimation of youthful ways of libido occupation which were entirely normal but which for the adult are no longer of value. These regressive infantile desires and fantasies, now alive and striving for satisfaction are converted into symptoms and in these surrogate forms obtain a certain gratification when creating the external manifestations of the neurosis. Thus, Jung departs from the traditional psychoanalytic viewpoint of emphasizing psychic experience or what point of fixation in childhood the patient is suffering. Jung talks of the present duty or task the patient is avoiding or what obstacle in his life's path he is able to overcome. It is interesting to note that many of Jung's patients were older people. By concentrating on current events in their lives, he was able to extend his theories to the treatment of older people where infantile and chronologically distant psychological material may have been lost. In his concepts of psychological determinism, the value of the conscious mind and thought and in his empirical development of a dynamic theory of life, Jung definitely reached the older segment of the population.

## LEWIN AND FIELD THEORY

Although Lewin's theory* seems to be appropriate for an analysis of the aging personality, there have been surprisingly few extensions made of his topological and vector constants for the purpose of studying the aging process. These extensions have primarily concerned attitudinal development during the later years. Lewin regards the life space of an older person as a great number of clearly differentiated regions within his psychological environment but especially within his personal region. "As one grows older the variety of his activities, emotions, needs, information, and social relationships increases at least up to a certain age. Thereafter, the versatility of his behavior may show a contraction." The inner state of the aged person can be characterized as one in which no strong and effective tensions arise because the barriers between the different regions have become too rigid or the general energy level has been significantly lowerd. Thus, it may be inferred that older persons may become more easily irritated by a loss of equilibrium and may not anticipate as well as younger people the correct moment for tension reduction in order to perform actions.

The studies of Kounin on rigidity, age, and feeblemindedness are probably one of the best translations of vector constants into personality research. Kounin constructed five hypotheses: "Other things being equal, the older and/or more feeble-minded an individual:

1. The less effect a change of state in one region will have upon the state of neighboring regions.
2. The less likely he is to be in an overlapping situation.
3. The more difficulty he will have in performing a task which requires him to be influenced by more than one region.
4. The more likely he is to structure a new field which is perceptively ambiguous into a relatively large number of separate independent regions.
5. The less easily he can perform a task which requires that he restructure a given field" (3) .

---

*Very generally, this theory regards the behavior of a person at a given moment as a function of the coexisting facts within his life space and his psychological field.

## ORGANISMIC VIEW

Organismic theory and personology involve the organismic views of Goldstein, Scheerer, and Gelb who investigated the effect of brain injury on personality and also the reasons for "concrete and abstract" thinking. In their discussions, they allude to the experiments on elderly of Thaler. Thaler observed that there is a marked change toward concrete behavior above the age of 60. She states, "They may try to adjust by sheer attempts to recognize aspects of their environment and be unable to form inferences and conceptually interpret what is going on around them. These aged persons may feel there is only one meaning to a situation and hence have the rigidity so often attributed to the elderly" (4).

## ROLE THEORY

Two kinds of studies have been undertaken in the area of role theory as related to the aged. One has been the perception and evaluation of the roles of the aged as viewed by different groups of the total population and under varying social conditions. The other is the actual roles which the aged take themselves.

Role psychologists assume that a person's adjustment is dependent on the number of roles he can enact. A maladjusted older person is one who did not acquire adequate roles for old age during his younger years. The conflicts are of two kinds: the self role conflict where there is conflict between the perceived self and the role one is supposed to play as an older person. These conflicts are very similar to ego defense mechanisms. The second kind of role is the role-role conflict which refers to behavior deviations and is not particularly indigenous to the aged.

Tuckman and Lorge found that people who use chronological age as a criterion of aging and who state a relatively low chronological age for its beginning or whose own age is closer to the age they conceive as the beginning of old age subscribe more to stereotypes about old people than those who have different views.

Chronological age is a poor index of aging since it does not take into account the range of individual differences among people. The years most frequently mentioned as the beginning of old age are between 60-65. Sarbin found that women related significantly more often than men to the role perceived according to the age of the person, while men emphasized the relationship between role and social situation.

There have been a number of anthropological reviews published on the role and treatment of older people and their attitudes toward age in other societies. In the second area mentioned, the Social Science Research Council's Committee on Social Adjustment in Old Age has given great impetus to the understanding of what roles older people play. In this connection, Pollack, Cavan, Albrecht, and Havighurst devoted a great deal of research to the roles and status of older people. The latter two defined 11 roles of older people and characterized them by various interests and activities thus getting the items of a questionnaire which they administered to 100 people over 65 years of age. This same questionnaire was used but modified in such a way that the subjects had to give their general approval of the various activities in which older persons may be engaged. They administered the questionnaire to almost a hundred persons of each decade above the age of 20. They found that the social evaluation of the activities of older people did not vary much below the age of 65.

The work of Blau and Phillips reinforces the concept of Sarbin. Blau says: "Age *identification* rather than actual age constrains older people to recognize changes in themselves and to perceive that the attitudes of others toward them have changes" (5). Among the objective changes, only retirement hastens the onset of old age, because it relates to social judgment rather than natural events and removes the subject from significant social communications and from the identifications with the younger age group.

## COMMUNICATION

The notions of people in psychology who are interested in information and feedback, primarily Bavelas, Horney, Norman, Festinger, and Osgood, again are primarily of peripheral relationship to the aging process, although there is a fertile field for future investigators. The work of Osgood has an interesting bearing on the psychology of aging. Osgood differentiates between the decoding and encoding stage of the organization of a behavioral act. The decoding stage denotes the process by which physical energies of the environment are interpreted by the organism and in the encoding stage the intentions of the organism are turned again into environmental events. In this "environmental inversion and eversion," the process is divided into organizational levels of "projective" (the relaying of receptor and muscle events to the brain), intellectual (the organization of these events), and representation (the termination of decoding and the beginning of encoding). It may be in the transmission of events and their external representation that future research in the study of aging lies, since it is in these complex psychic processes and their symbolic analysis that perhaps there is a breakdown during the aging process. Information theory analysis might provide a measure of how far a subject was deviating from conditioning probabilities and just how much, if any, older subjects do more than younger. This is particularly true in the area of expectancies and ignoring legitimate contextural possibilities.

## LEARNING THEORY AND THE AGING PROCESS

A word should be said here concerning learning theory in the broad context of personality development. Various personality theories touch tangentially on the problems of old age, but learning theory is an approach which takes the time variable into account.

### Hull

Hull, in his drive, cue, response, and reinforcement concepts, extended these concepts to the adjustment of his behavioral laws to the difference in species and individuals, although according to most experts he has not done this convincingly. He has not demonstrated whether individual differences can be explained by the variability in the individual's innate equipment or by deviations in the environmental influences. This may be due to the amount and kinds of cues presented, the reinforcement given, and the subservient response pattern and habits developed. More research must be done on the development of cue-response bonds over long time intervals and to individual differences in part or total number of stimuli previously presented.

## Guthrie

Guthrie's emphasis is on receptors, a connecting nervous system and muscles and glands. The movements and acts of the person are primarily of interest for psychological analysis. An act consists of movements. It is a class of movements defined by an end result which in a learning situation becomes associated with stimulus patterns. Riegel verified experimentally some of Guthrie's concepts relating to redundancy. He reasoned that older persons were relatively favored over younger if the tasks require the use of redundant information. He investigated verbal achievement of older persons by administering 5 multiple choice tests (synonym, antonym, selection, classification, and analogy) to 74 persons above the age of 65 and to 56 persons with an average age of 18.6 years. He reasoned that associations between words which are linguistically and logically related to each other should become strengthened during life by the continuous accumulation of information and by the adaptation of the person to general linguistic patterns. Therefore, tasks in which use of these associations can be made should reveal some advantage for people who had because of their age had more experiences of this kind. He found that the achievement of older persons on verbal tests decrease in the order: synonym, antonym, selection, classification, and analogy tests. The connection of this research with Guthrie's theory may be suggestive of future research and interpretations of the aging personality.

## Other Perceptual Theories

Learning and personality theories which have stressed primarily perceptual reorganization have been discussed* previously and have particular geriatric significance since many older people have their difficulty in the restructuring and reorganization of material. The conditions which seem to give the aged difficulty are tasks involving speed where there is little time for preliminary

*See pp. 23-27.

examination of materials. Just why this is so is not yet known.

## Maturation — Degeneration

The maturation — degeneration theory states quite simply that learning increases up to a certain age because of the organic growth of the nervous system and conversely there is a degeneration at the later end of life. A variant of this degenerative hypothesis is that learning decreases because of the loss of "plasticity" of the nervous system. There is an assumption that because the behavior of aged people is rigid, the nervous system is rigid which may not be necessarily so.

## Transfer of Training

Allusions have been made previously to the transfer of training and aging.** It has been shown rather convincingly that an individual so builds up habit strength that it governs his mode of operations over a wide variety of tasks, but strangely enough these learned procedures often persist to a point where they completely impede progress. Thus faced with a new situation, an individual considers only a limited range of possibilities and thus engages in those in which he has gained proficiency and which he has found profitable in the past, and these reinforced methods will take precedence over all others. This explains in part the difficulty which older people have in adapting to new situations and tasks.

## Retroactive and Proactive Inhibition

Systematic experience and experiments have shown that learning is influenced by antecedent experiences and there are differences in initial learning speeds according to the similarity and meaning of a task with a subject's previous learning. However, once the task has been learned, previous experience is not so important. Since learning in the aged is extremely important, particularly in educational and employment situations, and since the storage phase of the aged has been long, it is important to know just what influence this proactive phase of learning has upon future learning. As yet, our knowledge of this in the aged is rudimentary, but experiments by such people as Gladis and Braun

---

**See p. 28.

(7) are shedding light on this important problem with the aged.

## RECENT THEORIES

### Transactional Analysis

While the theory of transactional analysis is not directly related to gerontology, the division of the ego states into Parent, Adult, and Child is based partially on chronology. Berne*, in presenting his original classification framework, postulated that childhood ego states exist as relics in the grown-up. Berne further asserted the existence of two psychic organs: a neopsyche and an archeopsyche; the adult and child, respectively. It is the neopsyche organ which can become the parent or adult; and, the juncture at which geriatrics is involved. In old age, the adult takes over and becomes fixed, but as can be seen in the following pages, there are regressions to the child (archeopsyche) and introjection of parental figures (neopsyche).*

### Environmental Influences

The importance of early habits and their modification in later life, the generality and specificity of these habits and the importance of early deprivation are extremely important in the study of the aging process. Experimental work by Hebb, Tenbergen, and Himwich shows that the effect of restricting the environment in early life has been to depress learning in later life. At the conclusion of their review upon the effects of early experience upon the behavior of animals, Beach and Jaynes state that this influence is manifest in three ways:

1. Habits formed in early life persist in adult behavior.
2. Early perceptual learning affects adult behavior insofar as early experience structures the individual's perceptive capacities.
3. There are critical periods in the development of each.

So far, most of the experimental work has been in the area of animal research and much more is needed using human subjects.

---

*Berne, Eric, *Transactional Analysis in Psychotherapy*, New York: Grove Press, 1961.

Gendlin and Rychlak (1970) report that recently various systems of treatment have been proliferating in great numbers, but altogether they show 3 themes. First they are moving away from elaborate internal concepted nets and toward a more general "spirit" to which a variety of techniques can be attached. Second they are emphasizing brief interventions aimed at specific problems, rather than deep dynamic therapy aimed at reordering a life. Finally these new therapies take patients through small specific steps at treatment or even packaging the treatment in games or "homework" the patient can do himself. One of the more recent concepts is "behavior modification." Behavior therapy is essentially divided into 4 major techniques—positive reenforcement, desensitization, adversive procedures and modeling. There has been a great deal of success of these behavior modification procedures with the aged. A group of behaviorally oriented investigators intent on cure began developing programs only a few years after the socially oriented milieu theorists. These programs became very popular in the geriatric program in New York State and it was introduced in all mental hospitals, (New York Times 1971) and the programs have spread to other mental hospitals in other states.

## BIBLIOGRAPHY

1. Freud, Sigmund: On Psychotherapy — Collected Papers, Vol. 1. London, Hogarth Press, 1904; p. 288.
2. Erikson, E. H.: Identity and the Life Cycle. New York, International Universities Press, 1959, p. 98.
3. Kounin, J. S.: Experimental studies of rigidity. Character and Personality, 9:191, 251-282, 1941.
4. Thaler, Margaret: Relationships among Wechsler, Weigl, Rorschach, EEG findings and abstract — Concrete behavior in a group of normal aged subjects. *J. Gerontology, 11:*404-9, 1957.
5. Blau, Zena: Changes in status and age identification. Am. Sociol. Rev, *21:* 203, 1956.
6. Riegel, Klaus F.: A study of verbal achievements of older persons. J. Gerontol., *14:*453-456, October, 1959.
7. Gladis, M., and Braun, H. W.: Age differences in transfer and retroaction as a function of intertask response similarity. J. Exper. Psychol., *55:* 25-30, 1958.

8. Beach, F. A., and Jaynes, J.: Effects of early experience upon behavior of animals. Psychol. Bull., *51:* 239-263, 1954.
9. Gendlin, E. and Rychlak, S.: Psychotherapeutic Processes Annual Review of Psychology, 1970, 21 (from articles) Psychosomatic Treatment of the Aged by Gottesman, Leonore E.; Quarterman, Carole; and Cohen, Gordon H.: Psychology of Adult Development and Aging, edited by Eisdorfer, Carl and Lawton, M. Powell copyright 1973 by American Psychological Association, reprinted by Permission.
10. Berne, Eric: Transactional Analysis in Psychotherapy, New York, Grove Press 1961.

## General References

1. Freud, Sigmund: The Basic Writings of Sigmund Freud, A. A. Brill (ed.). New York, Modern Library, 1938.
2. Guthrie, E. R.: The Psychology of Learning. New York, Harper and Rowe, 1935.
3. Hull, C. L.: Principles of Behavior. New York, Appleton-Century Crofts, 1943.
4. Kretschmer, E.: Physique and Character. New Jersey, Harcourt, Brace and World, 1926.
5. Lewin, Kurt: Field Theory in Social Science, Darwin Cartwright (ed.). New York, Harper, 1951.

# Chapter III

## PSYCHOLOGICAL ASPECTS

### GENERAL CONSIDERATIONS

THE TASK OF assessing any ongoing human process, whatever it might be, is difficult at best; in the field of human behavior it becomes particularly difficult. Human beings react to stimuli, both internal and external, interact with others about them, and find themselves in fields of all sorts of transactional possibilities. These call for observational powers by the student of human behavior which may soon become outmoded even at their transcription. This is especially true in something as nebulous as the aging process. However, psychological description and assessment must nevertheless be pursued with whatever techniques are at hand, if we are to understand the entire process. It is important in those aspects of behavior that show change with age to ascertain both the *timing* and the *regularity* of these events. Regularity of timing is seen in many of the biological phenomena of life, e.g., the heart beat, contraction of the intestines, bowel movements, eye blink, menstruation, etc. Periodic biological rhythmic events range from a fraction of a second to months in length of cycle. While the biological systems return to their original phases, the organism as a whole moves forward in time. As the organism moves forward, relationships change between the biological subsystems, their periodic timing and human behavior. Thus, because of degeneratives changes in the vascular system, we get changes in memory and learning; changes in the auditory and visual systems bring about changes in various kinds of perception, etc. This is quite different from the biological influences in behavior in the young adult and child, inasmuch as the process in the older adult is catabolic or destructive while that in the younger is anabolic or constructive but this catabolic process in the older individual is not as potent as originally believed.

## Individual Differences

While there are certain behavioral patterns common to aging in humans, there are also wide individual differences *within* humans in their psychological characteristics in the aging process around the average age trend. There are also individual differences between species, but if a human being lives long enough he will show age characteristics of his species, but there is the possibility that the differences within the species (i.e., older human beings) may be greater than the differences between comparable ages in different species.*

A behavioral conception of aging must take into account various kinds of psychological functions such as age differences in perceptional and sensory functions, learning and memory, problem solving and thinking, psychomotor skills, motivation and the general problem of psychologically helping older people in a world of leisure and work with whatever tools may be at hand.

## THINKING, INTELLIGENCE AND PROBLEM SOLVING

### Thinking

An exact definition of thinking has never been devised, but it seems to be associated with ability to solve various kinds of abstract problems and an ability to communicate these solutions to others. Thinking is closely related to intelligence, and is, as a matter of fact, considered to be one of the elements of intelligence, primarily in terms of *kinds* of thinking, e.g., abstract thinking, concrete thinking, etc. If we again define thinking in terms of what "thinking tests" measure, just as intelligence might be defined as what intelligence tests measure, then thinking may be broadened to the ability to draw inferences, draw conclusions from syllogisms, evaluate arguments, weigh evidence and draw

---

*In species other than man, because of the hazards of the environment, many species of animals will die before reaching their age of peak fertility. However, under favorable laboratory conditions, these animals do reach senescence and exhibit definite biological and psychological characteristics.

deductions. The Watson and Glaser Critical Thinking Appraisal is a test which purports to evaluate such psychological functions. This test (1) was administered to 480 subjects age 12-80. There was a marked difference in the test results of the older and younger subjects. There were two reasons for poor performance of the older subjects. The first was the "inflexibility" of the older group. This inflexibility seems to be related to a disintegration of work methods in various mental skills and a decline in the problem solving orientation in the higher cognitive processes associated with aging which may be related to disuse after leaving school. This was evidenced on the test by a tendency to choose absolute categories of true and false rather than considering alternative answers. The second difference between the older and younger subjects was a lower "objectivity." The older subjects tend to rely more on past experience for answers which colors their logical thinking and replies are based on attitude rather than analysis. Older subjects are in a sense influenced more by emotion rather than logical analysis, and have difficulty sorting out relevant items (1), the inhibition is caused by personal association.

Jerome (2) reports a study where two sets of subjects in a wide age range pressed buttons that illuminated lights in a sequence; the job was to integrate in an orderly arrangement the sequentially elicited light key pairings. The problems were those of logical problem solving which were given at four levels of difficulty in an ascending order of complexity. If the subject failed to solve a problem, he was given another problem of equal difficulty. The younger subjects were markedly superior to the older. The older subjects were not able to identify the problem early, they had a haphazard method of search behavior, a high degree of redundancy in the inquiry of the problem, and a disinclination to keep notes.

In a later study, Young (1966) using problems of the same type as Jerome, devised tasks of 4 levels of difficulty with 3 problems at each level. When a subject failed to solve a problem, he was told the strategy to the solution of the problem. All the young subjects were able to solve the third problem at the first three levels of difficulty and all but one solved the last problem at the most difficult level while only 4 of the older subjects reached solutions for the 4 levels of difficulty. The old required many more inquiries when they reached solutions, even when they reached solutions, and were unable to apply the solution strategy.

From the latest studies on problem solving with the aged, it appears that older people are impaired in the processing of information, in arriving at a solution and obtaining information for the solving of problems.

## Intelligence

Intelligence tests in general can predict how well an individual can do in school and the professions but not in business. The results of studies on intelligence tests indicate that results are subject to both positive and negative effects of aging. In the first 20 years, the results are chiefly positive; in senescence the results are chiefly negative. These later negative changes may be due to cerebral involutional or secondarily involutional causes (due to aging in some other structure than the brain), decreasing motivation, habits interfering with testing or a combination of these.

## History of Intelligence Testing on Older People

Foster and Taylor (3) compared a group of hospital patients 50 years of age and older, a younger group and a group of school children on the Yerkes-Bridges Point Scale, an intelligence test devised in the 1920's. The authors found that there was a decline in scores with age which they attributed not only to the loss of intelligence but also to reduced interest and alertness and a lack of practice in the functions sampled. The decreases with age were in the following areas.

1. Drawing from memory.
2. Putting three words in one sentence.
3. Rephrasing dissected sentences.
4. Word association (number of words in three minutes).

The tests which indicated an increased score with age were:

1. Vocabulary.
2. Comprehension of questions.
3. Judgement of absurdities.

Beeson (4) found that vocabulary function held up with age but also found a decline in other kinds of functions viz.

1. Analysis, synthesis, and arithmetic reasoning.
2. Inventiveness, ingenuity, and imagination.
3. Immediate visual memory and perception.

During the First World War, Yerkes (5) reported on officers and their decrement of the total score on the Army Alpha according to age. There was a marked decrement in scores beyond the age 30 and most marked in the 51-60 group.

In a study by Willoughby (7) on items from the Army Alpha and Beta, the National Intelligence Test and the Stanford Achievement Test, the following functions were found to decline at the following ages: Analogies, symbol-digit substitution, symbol-series completion, and number-series completion at age 20; arithmetic reasoning and vocabulary hold up well at all ages, including well past 50.

Walter Miles used an abbreviated 15-minute form of the Otis and tested 566 subjects in the age range 20-80. He classified the results in terms of seven intelligence groups. Marked age changes were seen in each decade.

**Recent Studies**

Studies of the gifted by Terman show interesting results in ·the higher age group. The members of Terman's group were born between 1903 and 1920, and tested within the top 1% on the Stanford-Binet. A Concept Mastery Test was devised for use with this group which assessed the subject's knowledge of concepts in many different fields by an analogies test and a synonym-antonym test. The test was given and in two equivalent subforms in 1939-40 and 12 years later. Although most other studies show a decline in reasoning by analogy in the upper age group, Terman's subjects showed a *delayed* decline, that is, the decline in this function came well after the decline in other groups, indicating that in respect to these functions a group as exceptional as Terman's retain these functions longer than more·average groups.

The Progressive Matrices Test is a non-verbal test requiring logical reasoning by analogy. It is purported to test a subject's intellectual activity independent of language or knowledge acquired. Studies with this test show that in most cases a peak is reached at 13-14, much earlier than most normative studies of intellectual functions, and the decline is gradual after 30.

## AGE AND DIFFERENTIAL FUNCTIONS

### Perception and Dexterity

Bilash and Zubek (6) found that the functions of perception and dexterity decline from the teens to the 70's whereas comprehension and verbal fluency hold up until the mid-forties.

Corso has published the most recent review of the sensory changes. He came to the conclusion that the principal mechanism involved in sensory changes of the aged are both neural and non-neural. The neural loss is irreversible and there is a general reorganization of the peripheral and central nervous system. Differential susceptibility to certain illusions, decreased ability to abstract information from embedded figures, difficulties in handling irrelevant stimuli and changes in information processing and signal detection seem to occur in the older person. Very little is known at this date about the compensatory abilities of neuronel feedback network. Thus in older people, even if some networks are lost, the possibility of applying modern feedback procedures to transfer the lost functions to another network is an interesting idea for innovative researchers.

### Vocabulary

Vocabulary tests seem to maintain their level with age better than most other functions assessed by intelligence tests. It is interesting to note that within a group of a given age, vocabulary has been shown to be highly correlated with overall intelligence test scores. Over a wide age range, however, vocabulary scores have much greater validity because other functions decline with age, while the vocabulary scores remain approximately the same.

The most recent work on the WAIS vocabulary has been done by Botwinick, West and Storandt (1975). 107 subjects—between 16 and 20 subjects in each age decade, 20s through 70s. The subjects were independent, community dwelling volunteers drawn from church and community organizations, evening school classes, an apartment complex for retired people and neighbors and acquaintances of the authors. The mean level of education of the youngest age decades were 14-15 years and in the two oldest decades (60s and 70s), the education level was approximately 11 years. The vocabulary test responses as traditionally scored were compared to these same responses when scored for finer nuances of understanding as determined by the criterion of superior synonyms. The experimenters hypothesized that the aged would show a greater deficit pattern in the superior synonym context. The results partly supported this hypothesis, i.e. the aged do have a deficit pattern but it was not clear whether the aged cannot or do not give synonym responses as readily as the young. The authors conclude that this may be a preference rather than an age limitation of intellectual ability.

**Information**

Figure 3 shows the age changes in the composition of test scores at successive ages for the Army Alpha. It will be noted that beyond age 50, the vocabulary and information tests contribute more than 40% to the total test score while in adolescence it is only about 30%. Information and vocabulary are influenced by experience and accumulation of knowledge and favor older people in comparison with younger.

Figure 3.

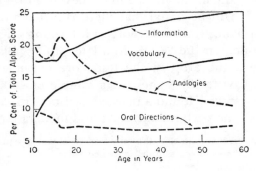

**Other Functions**

Such tasks as definitions, verbal understanding, naming coins, counting pennies, stand up rather well with age. Those that do not stand up with age are those that require novel or new situations, ingenuity, or persistent effort.

## COGNITIVE FUNCTIONS AND STUDIES ON THE WECHSLER-BELLEVUE

The variables of age and previous training have been touched upon tangentially by Tolman in his means-end readiness theory of cognitive readiness, but he has not elaborated upon this theory in detail. Tolman evolved a theory of "molar" behavior as opposed to the "molecular" approach, which defines complex behavior reduced to configurations of elementary units. Tolman has also defined variables which influence cognitive processes, such as previous training, hormone conditions, heredity, and age. However, he does not elaborate in detail both the importance and relationship of those variables but does mention age and past training. The work of Jones on intelligence and problem solving, Jerome on learning, and Welford on psychomotor performance, are a few who elaborated on this area of cognitive functioning. A number of psychologists, viz. Balinsky, Goldfarb, Birren, Cohen, and Riegel, experimented with factor analysis of the Wechsler-Bellevue Intelligence Test with older people.

In the initial standardization of the Wechsler-Bellevue in 1944, a stratified sample was used based on the occupational distribution of the U. S. census. Figure 4 indicates the verbal and performance scores of 1751 persons in the initial standardization on the basis of the mean and standard deviation for the age group 20-25 years. It will be noted that there is a sharp drop at age 25 in the performance scale and more of a leveling off at that age in the verbal scale. On the WAIS, in a later study (1951) in Kansas City, Missouri, the drop in the test score began at a later age. Corsini and Fassett (8) in testing a sample of 4000 prisoners at San Quentin prison* found a marked decline with age in three of the subtests of the performance scale and moderate decline in two

---

*Corsini and Fassett maintain that the only way to obtain a representative sample is in prison, and the "forced sample" obtained there overcame the difficulties of cooperation at the upper age levels.

of the subtests of the verbal scale while there was an increase in the information scale (Figs. 5 and 6).

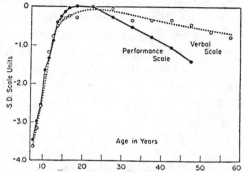

Figure 4. Age means in the Wechsler-Bellevue, in terms of the mean and standard deviation for ages 20-25.

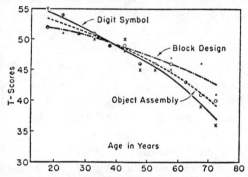

Figure 5. Age means in three Wechsler-Bellevue subtests, in terms of T-scores for young adults (a prison sample). (Adapted from data furnished by R. J. Corsini.)

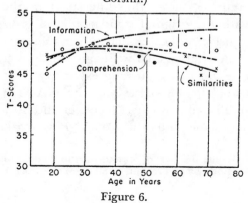

Figure 6.

Balinsky, using the Thurstone Centroid method factor, factor analyzed the WAIS, in which he divided age groups into years, 9, 15, 25-29, 35-44, and 50-59, he found that the memory factor appeared only in ages 25-29 and 35-44, that there was a "g" factor analagous to Speakman's "g" which was found in the 9 year age group, then is hidden but appears again but not until about ages 50-59;* the verbal and performance factors are the most constant, and that the same factors do not appear at each level.

Cohen factor analyzed the 1955 edition of the WAIS. He divided his sample into four age groups — 18-19, 25-34, 45-54, and 60-75 years and over. He found that in the age group 60-75 the memory factor attracted large parts of the variance of the "g" factor which showed high loading in all the subtests, and accounted for about half the subtest variance, and therefore older people depended heavily on retention and memory.

Birren factor analyzed the WAIS by means of Thurstone's Centroid method. His subjects were 90 people between 60-74. He found four factors — verbal comprehension (V), perceptual closure (C), memory (M), and induction (I). Birren considered V & C as a combination representing stored knowledge and experience of older people which is very important to their achievement, as opposed to immediate understanding and learning during the test situation.

In a study by Birren using the WAIS on 47 men over the age of 65 who were divided into 2 groups, those regarded in optimum health and those who had subclinical or asymptomatic disease (20), there were wide differences in the two groups' verbal intelligence test scores. Figure 7 shows the differences in the scores and a comparison with the original standardization group. This study, using the Wechsler, indicates that when there are physiological changes in the body associated with aging such as cerebral circulation, there is intellectual regression especially those involving the kinds of items on the verbal scale of the WAIS.

In an unpublished study by Kleemeier and his associates, their data shows that some individuals may show marked stability of

---

*This apparently refutes the view of Speakman who thought his "g" factor would increase during adulthood and remain stable until the onset of senility.

mental functioning in the later years whereas other persons show a rather precipitous decline. Precipitous decline in mental functioning in the aged is likely to be indicative of short survival.

The most recent findings on intellectual functioning using the WAIS among a group of relatively healthy community volunteers is based on a longitudinal interdisciplinary study at Duke University Center for the Study of Aging and Human Development. The testing involved 224 subjects in the 60-79 (one group 60-69 and another group 70-79) age range, 98 of whom completed four examinations during a ten year follow-up period. Intellectual changes among the survivors of the 10 year study as well as the intellectual performance of the subjects who were lost to the program before the fourth evaluation were examined.

The initial overall intellectual level of these subjects was positively correlated with survivorship. The total sample including survivors and non-survivors pooled together showed an *increase* over time in contrast to the decrement noted among the survivors and non-survivors separately. The survivors who were initially examined at 60-69 had a significant decrement over time in the performance area which was reflected in 2.6 mean drop in their over-all scores. The survivors examined at ages 70-79 had a significant loss in all areas. The subjects in the middle I.Q. range who were initially tested at ages 60-69 years had a slight, significant decline in the performance area while those in the age range 70-79 had a decrement in all areas. Those who had a high I.Q. in the 70-79 age range had a loss in the performance area. The people with low I.Q.s at both age levels had a slight but non-significant loss over time. Thus the decline noted in the performance area among the entire sample (independent of the initial I.Q. level) of survivors first examined at ages 60-69 could be primarily attributed to those subjects in the middle I.Q. range at this age. The significant losses in all areas observed among the entire sample of survivors initially tested at age 70-79 could be primarily attributed to those subjects in the middle I.Q. range with the high I.Q. subjects also accounting for some of the decline.

In another study at the Duke University Center for the Study of

Aging and Human Development, a 15 year follow-up study was done on 37 non-surviving and 66 surviving participating aged individuals, testing the hypothesis that intellectual changes are related to nearness of death. The WAIS was also used in this study as the criterion of intellectual performance. The results show that survivors and non-survivors did not differ significantly in test scores. Among the non-survivors those nearest death tended to have the lowest scores; however there was significant relationship between actual scores and nearness to death. Among the non-survivors the group that died within 13-32 months after testing had greater losses than did the survivors and the major portion of observed loss occurred approximately 7-10 years before death. In contrast the group that died within one year after the final test had intellectual changes that were not markedly different from the survivors. Thus some, but not all, individuals experience a marked intellectual loss before death. Previous investigations have shown that the initially less able intellectually tend to die sooner than the initially more able non-survivors who sustained both acute and chronic illnesses had a greater intellectual loss than their counterparts with chronic disease but no serious acute illnesses, suggesting that acute illness superimposed on chronic illness had a significant effect on intellectual deterioration of the aged.

A German revision of the Wechsler-Bellevue has been accomplished and a standardization done on subjects 10-60. Riegel (9) , in analyzing this data, states that in the majority of the subtests the German averages rise more slowly in adolescence, reach a later peak and with the exceptions of information, comprehension and similarities decline more slowly after age 30 than the American sample.

Riegal factor analyzed the German standardization. He subdivided his samples into four age groups — 20-34, 35-49, 50-64, and 65-75 using the centroid method as well as Hotelling's principal component. His results were quite similar to Birren's, i.e., achievements during old age are determined by general and redundant experience and less so by specific knowledge characteristic of verbal learning during youth.

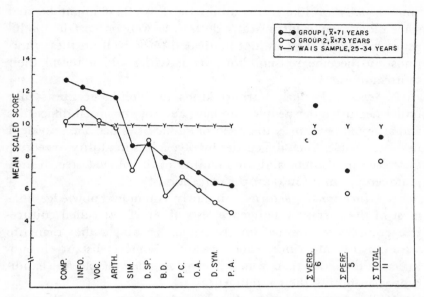

Figure 7. Comparison of the subtest scores of the Wechsler Adult Intelligence Scale for three groups of subjects: young standardization group, healthy elderly men (group 1), and elderly men with mild asymptomatic disease (group 2). The expected mean value for young adults is ten on each subtest. *Source:* Birren, J. E., Bulter, R. N., Greenhouse, S. W., Sokoloff, L., and Yarrow, Marian R.: *Human Aging.* Washington, D.C., Government Printing Office, Public Health Publication No. 986, 1963, p. 151.

Insofar as the Wechsler-Bellevue and WAIS is concerned, age has a positive relationship for some subtests (information and vocabulary) and a negative relationship in others (digit symbol, picture arrangement, and picture completion). However, there are many factors which must be taken into account in the assessment of the intelligence of older people.

*1. Motivation.* Beyond the age of 60, motivation seems to play a big part in the scores on intelligence tests. There seems to be a definite motivational loss beyond this age point. There is a slower decline at the upper end of the intelligence distribution which may be related to a slower rate of change in motivation with intellectually superior people. It should be remembered that it is difficult to remember which is the chicken and which the egg.

Since usually we like to do things we do well, it might be that since older people intrinsically do not do well on certain intelligence functions, they are not motivated to do well on these functions and become resistant towards activities which reveal their shortcomings.

2. *Sensory Factors.* Various kinds of intelligence tests may undermeasure older people who have auditory or visual difficulties and as noted previously these sensory difficulties become prevalent in older people. Such difficulties involve a loss in ability to receive the necessary content and the inability of the older testee to integrate sensory input into proper perceptions.

3. *Educational Factors.* It is fairly common knowledge that most of the current intelligence tests (even the so-called culture-free group) are oriented toward school learning rather than life achievement, and since school learning is more distant chronologically for older than younger people; older people are handicapped in testing their intelligence.

4. *Speed.* In those tests where time is important, older persons may be handicapped. Older people are used to taking "deliberate aim" and are usually more impressed by caution than younger. Those tests where quick and "snap" judgements are at a premium may favor younger people since, the older people's "life style" is not oriented toward taking chances and gambling,* whereas the younger person may be oriented in the school milieu to attempt tasks where there are time limits with quick starts and stops. Miles (10), in reporting on results with the Otis given without time limits to 433 subjects as compared with the same test in alternate form administered under standard time limits, found that the decline from early maturity to the 60's was .46 S. D. units without time limits and .76 S. D. units under standard conditions so that 1/3 of the decline in this age interval was due to loss in speed.

5. *Psychometric Problems.* It has been widely suggested that

*In a recent study (1975), Birkhill, and Schaie investigated employing 56 females and 32 males with a mean age of 73 years. Cautiousness was manipulated by urging pretest instruction conditions involving 2 levels of risk and response omission when taking the Primary Mental Abilities Test. The results clearly indicate that performance in intelligence tests is influenced by various situational variables involving motivational components. Those subjects exposed to low risk conditions performed much better on cognitive tasks than those exposed to high risk conditions.

different kinds of functions and criteria should be utilized in constructing tests, and especially intelligence tests for older people. Kaplan (11) says "Intelligence tests encompass only a limited range of mental abilities and either undervalue or ignore some of the abilities which are most important in daily life. For example, they do not adequately provide for the measurement of originality and the higher forms of judgment." In some instances, tests do actually favor older persons because of the weighting of experience rather than ability and secondly more superior samples are drawn at successive ages. Probably future tests and research will use age curves based on functions similar to Thurstone's primary mental abilities elicited from factor analyses made at a series of ages.

*6. Creativity and Age.* Dennis (12) has tabulated by decades of life the scientific articles of 156 well known scientists who lived to age 70 or beyond, 56 of whom lived to age 80 and beyond. He found a relatively small decrease in rate of publication up to age 80. The decade of the 20's is the least productive, the scientists publishing less than half as much as they did 50 years later. The decades of the 40's and 50's were the most productive and about equal. In the 60's and 70's, the output is respectively about 80% and 65% of what it is during the peak decades. Dennis found that it was possible to predict a scientist's productivity in his 60's and 70's from his record in the 40's and 50's. The correlations between pairs of these decades range from 50-85, adjacent decades yielding the highest values.

Lehman made an age classification for nearly 1000 contributions sufficiently noteworthy to be mentioned in a history of chemistry. The highest proportion occurred when the contributors were in the age bracket 30-34. Two-thirds of the contributions were between 40 and 50% after age 60. These results indicate an early rather than a late peak of intellectual ability, and a subsequent decline. The peak of *scientific* and *artistic* achievement is expected later than the peak of intellectual growth. Results for other scientific fields, painting and literary and musical productions, and for practical inventions and chess are similar to that of chemistry.

7. *Sex Differences.* It is well known that women outlive men. However, the data regarding sex differences and age with respect to mental abilities in the U. S. is almost non-existent. A study in Japan (13) indicates that in 12 intelligence subtests women score lower than men at all ages. The data even indicates a sex difference in favor of men at all ages on verbal tests while in the U. S. it appears that women outperform men on verbal tests.

In general, it can be gathered from existing evidence that there is no gradual decline with age in general mental ability. The primary aspect of mental performance that changes with age in most persons is that of slowing of speed of response. The average person in our society who grows older need not expect to show a typical deterioration of mental functioning in the later years. Limitations of mental functioning occurs rather precipitously in individuals over the age of 65 or 70 and is related to health status.

8. *Learning.* The relation of the aging process to learning theories is discussed on pages 27, 28.

Because of the decrease in sensory and perceptual acuity and physiological drives, learning facility decreases in older individuals. However, this is made up for by other factors. For example the novelty in a learning situation favors older persons.

Impairment in learning in older people vs. that in younger ones is most pronounced in terms of speed.* Older people need time to respond and adequate pacing is a mechanism by which age differences may be reduced. Since interference effects (retroactive inhibition)** assume greater prominence as age increases, any manipulation reducing interference keeps age differences to a minimum. In addition older people have difficulty acquiring stimuli due to degeneration of the perceptual processes. Reinforcement given to the individual for responding faster results in rapid and more accurate performance. Older people tend to make errors of omission rather than errors of commission. It is not clear whether this error performance is evidence of some response inhibition or may be due to a general cautiousness or reservation. The areas of concept formation, and decision making behavior in the elderly have not as yet been thoroughly explored.

* see P 46
**see P 29

9. *Animal Studies.* Stone (14), in his early studies with rats, using a multiple discrimination box, did not find age differences in learning in the rats between the ages of 31 days and 770 days. At each of the five check points in the discrimination box, the rat had to choose an exit through one of two windows. The correct window was that which was illuminated on a given trial. Birren (15) studied learning in a rat using a swimming tank. When animals are matched for initial ability to learn, reversal of a two choice situation does not produce interference in the older rat. The older rat, however, swims back and forth along the side wall of a tank and thus avoids a choice point. The experimenters interpreted this as a habit on the part of the older rat to cling to the wall as an affinity point. This, say the experimenters, is an example of an old habit pattern interfering with the learning process. Thus, the older rat seems to depend more upon touch and feeling sensation than the younger rat. However, in general, there was little evidence of deficit in the older rat and ability to learn a two choice T maze. Verzár-McDougall (16) had rats of different ages learn a multiple T maze to obtain a food reward. The criterion of learning was not more than three errors in three consecutive runs. In general, the older rats showed inferior learning in the maze, but half the rats in the age range of 12-27 months learned the maze just as well as the young adult rats 8-9 months old.

The studies of age and learning on rats indicate that while deficits in learning of older rats do occur, they are not uniform under all conditions and these deficits are due to such variables as perception, motivation, and senile debilitation which is not characteristic of all rats used in such experiments.*

10. *Interference (Inhibition) Effects.* Gladis and Braun (17) examined the effects of age on learning and recall of paired associ-

---

*Recent experiments on humans indicates that learning and short term retention improves for the old person when he says the material aloud. Arenberg has hypothesized that material presented visually in short term retention is converted to an auditory storage. In the older person, the effectiveness of this storage process is reduced, that is the elderly have difficulty converting visual input to auditory storage. Thus, responding vocally facilitates the auditory storage in older people. (Arenberg, David: Verbal learning and retention. *The Gerontologist*, 7:1, 10, March 1967.)

ates. Each subject learned an eight item paired associates word list. After this initial learning, the subjects learned paired associates with varying degrees of similarity in meaning to the original lists. Then, each subject relearned the original list of paired associates two minutes after he learned the interpolated lists of words of varying relationship to the original materials. The subjects ranged in age from 20-29, 40-49, and 60-72. Table 4 indicates the results. There seems to be a superiority in the absolute amount of transfer for the older subjects when the new scores are considered. However, there is a superiority in favor of youth when the scores are transformed to reciprocals and adjusted for vocabulary** and the rate of original learning.

TABLE 4
AVERAGE LEARNING RATE AND RECALL SCORES
FOR PAIRED ASSOCIATES IN SEVERAL AGE GROUPS

| Types of Score | Age Groups | | |
| | 20 to 29 | 40 to 49 | 60 to 72 |
| --- | --- | --- | --- |
| Mean raw scores: | | | |
| Original learning ................ | 14.8 | 19.7 | 23.3 |
| Interpolated learning ............ | 10.9 | 15.2 | 17.7 |
| Gains ........................... | 3.9 | 4.5 | 5.6 |
| Recall .......................... | 4.3 | 4.0 | 3.3 |
| Transformed scores: | | | |
| Original learning ............... | 79.98 | 59.65 | 53.30 |
| Interpolated learning ........... | 116.88 | 80.88 | 72.30 |
| Gains .......................... | 36.90 | 21.23 | 19.00 |
| Adjusted scores: | | | |
| Original learning ............... | 85.78 | 59.18 | 48.10 |
| Interpolated learning ........... | 112.23 | 83.48 | 73.81 |
| Gains .......................... | 26.45 | 24.30 | 25.71 |
| Recall .......................... | 3.90 | 4.14 | 3.52 |

*Source*: Gladis, M., and Braun, H. W.: Age differences in transfer and retroaction as a function of intertask response similarity. *J. Exper. Psychol. 55*:25-30, 1958.

Ruch (18) tested the effects of age on reorganization of long established behavior patterns using a rotary pursuit task in which the subject followed a spot on a rotating phonograph-like disc with a stylus. In the first part of the study, direct vision was employed whereas in the other part of the study mirror vision requiring reorganization of visual motor habits was employed. Under the conditions of mirror reversal, the older subjects gave a relatively poorer performance than they did in the direct view situations. Thus, as expected, because of the consolidation of

**See pages 38, 39 for the relationship of vocabulary and age.

visual-motor habits of older persons, the mirror reversal produced a greater decrement in the performance of the older subjects.

The results of interference with older persons cited above were obtained under laboratory conditions. We still do not know the effects, for example, of long term past habits or present living and whether, in fact whether such habits do (and if they do, how much) interfere with present learning. It stands to reason that certain experiences will have a negative transfer situation in various learning situations, but we must await the results of long term longitudinal studies to verify these assumptions.

*11. Learning in Vocations and Occupations.* One of the essential differences in learning performance between the young and old is the amount that has to be retained or held in short term memory in learning. In older people, short term memory is most impaired in those tasks in which there is a continuous intermittent intake of information where there is *serial* response.* Various reasons have been ascribed. One of these is the physiological one that the difficulty in immediate memory is a result of deficiency in oxygen to the brain due to impaired circulation or altered brain metabolism, inability to encode a trace is an interference effect from the pattern of nerve activity. Both immediate and short term memory decline in the visual and auditory modalities occur, but visual memory seems to be more affected than auditory storage. Physiologically, experimentation seems to indicate molecular coding in the DNA-RNA matrix.** Older people also seem to learn more easily the essentials relevant to their needs, interests, and preservation and are likely to recall this data when confronted with the actual situation in which it can be applied.

The above observations have importance in retraining programs in industry and just how these retraining programs should be instituted since retraining of adult workers has become a major activity in industries subject to rapid technological change. It has been shown, again, for example, that older people show anxiety in learning situations particularly if they are placed in competitive positions, where younger people are included. While the young are undisturbed by errors which they apparently accept as a part

* See page 42, supra.
**See page 6, supra

of learning, the old are more reluctant to make mistakes.

The introduction of automation has placed a rather interesting cognitive cloud on the worker in an automated plant. He must enter (or return) to a classroom-like situation for retraining. Quite often in the automated industrial plants, the whole plant works as a unit, or not at all, requiring operators to depend on highly instrumental control systems, and to have knowledge about processes in all parts of the plant. Thus speed, strength, and dexterity are not as important as long term integration of abstract information and planning of strategy.

In studies of petroleum and telephone companies which have switched to automated processes, it has been shown that the older instrument workers in the petroleum industry do somewhat better in training courses than do the younger (19) but in a study of telephone workers where IBM cards were substituted for a form for marking of telephone numbers, the proportion of telephone trainees with above average scores for correct marking on the IBM card declined with increasing age (20). Evidently, in the type of performance required of telephone operators involving psychomotor coordination and speed, older workers find more difficulty.*

As stated previously** much of the difficulty in the learning of older people seems to be in the area of perception. The learning of older people in industrial situations is a complex one, but certain generalizations can be made. Older people learn best by methods which are adjusted to their own patterns and abilities. They should be presented material in such a way that will allow them to perceive *clearly* the *essentials* of the task involved. Clearly written instructions seem to be better than verbal ones. The rate or pace of instructions should be slowed down to enable the older industrial worker or trainee to fully comprehend as learning progresses. Learning by the activity method seems to be superior to that of memorizing. Spacing of training with definite pauses is important. Because of the difficulties older workers have with interference and unlearning, instructions and task should be clearly related to each other and ambiguities kept to a minimum. Attitudes also seem to be quite important. Discouragement and depression, two difficulties of older workers, should be avoided.

* See page 46
**See page 46

Finally, older workers as well as younger ones, do have individual differences and emphasis should be placed on training the individual worker.

## Motivation

The problem of motivation in the elderly is complicated by social demands, feedback and reinforcements. These change motivational patterns. The problem of securing a baseline for energy expenditure is another one which complicates assessment of motivation. For example, under specific test situations where the older person knows he is going to be tested, he may drive himself to such an extent that a false picture is given of his energy expenditure. Nevertheless, studies have been done under controlled conditions on both young and elderly subjects where a mild electric shock was administered to both sets of subjects when they evidenced a slower response to an auditory stimulus than had been evidenced with previous experiments. There was a decrease in reaction time for both groups with the older ones showing about the same decrement as the younger. In order to conteract the deficiencies of the formally set measurement situation, it has been proposed that studies be made of the older individuals self-oriented and self initiated activity by various kinds of observational techniques outside of the experimental situation, but up to now there have been very few such studies.

The motivational changes in age seems to be a conservative one, i.e., there is avoidance of risk, reduction of challenges to the mind and body and conservation of time and emotional energy. The latter is particularly true in the area of work habits and attitudes. For example, older people develop an adaptive economy in work such as resting in off periods while younger people may play at active games. In addition, the older person will start his job promptly, carry tasks through to conclusion, spend his work time systematically, and complete his work in spite of errors etc. Such factors are related partly to the intensity of motivation in particular situations and partly to the ability of the individual to organize his energy and activity patterns. Other individual factors in the older person's earlier experiences such as obsessive-compulsive tendencies (exhibited by an overemphasis on accuracy) and concern about making fools of themselves in the presence of their associates again complicates the whole assessment of motivation.

More specific areas of motivation are discussed on page 42.

### Interests and Age

Most of the studies of the changes of interests with age have come from the work of Strong. The greatest *range* of interests are among children of 9 years and there is a steady drop in the variety of interests until the age of 22. Brighter children in general have a greater variety of interests than do average children and boys more than girls. In general, as a person matures he pursues a smaller number of activities with more intensity and depth. Other kinds of shifts also occur, because of changes of appearance and physical capacities. For example, sports participants may become sports spectators. There is a tendency as people get older for them to become more interested in relatively solitary activities rather than those involving large groups. Older people's interests increase in the area of reading and decrease in the area of being amused. An interesting observation is that studies have shown that the average time spent in watching television remains about the same throughout the adult life span with older people liking variety and talent shows while younger ones are interested in serious drama and mystery programs. In general, however, once a person has reached maturity his interest patterns acquire stability in broad areas.

Strong, in a study of changes of interests with age, analyzed the results of the Strong Vocational Interest Blank on 2340 men varying in age from 20-59 years. On the whole, there were little changes with age in the proportion of likes and dislikes. The amount of change from 20-60 years was only 7.5%. Figure 8 shows the differential picture obtained when items are plotted against age. The reader will note that there is a distinction between active and competitive items and more sedentary and ·non-competitive activities. Items suggesting physical skill, daring or strenuous activity, changes or interference with established habits or cultural patterns, linguistic activities, and amusement decrease with age.

Liking for a particular occupation, activities involving reading, and solitary activities increase with age. In terms of specific items on the Strong Blank there is an increase in liking for magazines such as the National Geographic, for spending evenings at home, in art galleries, in making a speech, becoming secretary of a society. There is decreased interest in driving an automobile, in musical comedy, in playing tennis, and in exploring. Items such as listening to a symphony, reading detective stories, and being an undertaker show little change with age.

There is also indication from Strong's studies that what is liked most at 25 years is liked better with increasing age and what is liked less at 25 is liked still less with advancing age. If we identify interest in strenuous and dangerous activities as being

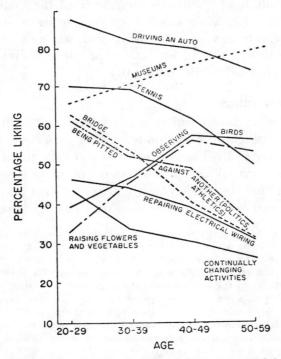

Figure 8. Changes with age in various interests as measured by the Strong Test (Strong, E. K.: *Change of Interest with Age.* Stanford, Calif., Stanford University Press, 1931). *Source:* Pressey, S. L., and Kuhlen, R. G.: *Psychological Development Through the Life Span.* New York, Harper & Row, 1957.

masculine, then males tend to become more feminine over the life span with females showing the greatest femininity of interest at about 13 with movement toward masculine interests until 19 and then more femininity until the 50's after which there is little change.

Participation in various activities and hobbies by older people is directly related to cultural and educational status.* For example, the amount of time spent loafing or doing nothing is much greater among laborers and unskilled workers who have retired than it is among educated persons.

What has been said of the interests of older people who are working does not necessarily hold in retirement. Hobby activities decline consistently from late adolescence through middle adulthood. After 50, hobby activities increase until the early 70's, and then decrease again. We are only beginning to learn the type and meaning of interests in retirement and we must make such interests more meaningful for retired people if they are to continue to feel wanted by the community.

### Attitudes and Values

In general, attitudes and values are developed as the result of a gamut of influences, e.g., family, groups in society, individual experiences and individual personalities and these influences cause a tremendous variety of opinions about other processes, objects and people. However, differences in attitudes have been found in age *groups* and between the sexes within any age group. Young

---

*Male members of a day center for senior citizens in New York City were administered the Strong Vocational Interest Blank in order to study the effects of age and retirement on interest patterns. All of the subjects were in the lower and lower-middle class, of the Jewish faith, and homogeneous with respect to country of origin, work experience and educational background. The patterns of findings indicated that younger retirants compared to older retirants, express stronger interest in solitary activities involving greater independence, prestige and material gain. The older retirants compared to the younger retirants showed stronger interest in social interactional activities and ones which involved supervisory responsibilities of a somewhat lower status level. Thus, among less wealthy and less educated older people, increasing years of retirement and age appear to be associated with a stronger interest in social activities and social participation. (Vogel, Bruce, S., Schell, Robert E.: Vocational interest patterns in late maturity and retirement: *Gerontol., 1:*23, 66-70, Jan. 1968.)

women tend to view older people's appearance more negatively than either young men or older men. Older men are generally regarded as being more submissive and less authoritative than older women, especially in very recent times where women have taken over many jobs thought previously only relegated to men. Here, there is a fundamental change in the role of the sexes in the later years. In his youth, a man is impelled toward action and achievement, and becomes increasingly power conscious. Psychological and physiological changes and loss of authority in retirement may place the male in his later years in a more dependent role than that of the women.

Kogan and Wallach (22) did a study on attitudes and values with age. The subjects were required to indicate their ratings of a list of concepts checking on a 7-point scale along dimensions: fair-unfair, strong-weak, active-passive, safe-dangerous. Older subjects of both sexes, interestingly enough, viewed the Negro and retirement more favorably than younger ones, and one might speculate that dependent people in a society (in this case the older subjects) have a favorable attitude toward deprived people (the Negro). The study also indicated that older men tend to have more favorable reaction to such concepts as "foreign" than younger men, while older women are more favorable than young women in evaluation of death, but less favorable in evaluation of love.

There is some indication that individuals with a high level of education and a relatively high socio-economic status are likely to possess greater internal and external resources so that regardless of age and retirement, highly uniform social participation patterns and interest may prevail. In those people with limited internal and external resources, we would find substantial differences in the strengths of various interests with age and retirement. In a study done at a day center for elderly citizens (23) in New York City, who were socio-economically in the lower and low-middle class, 39 subjects* were administered the Strong Vocational Interest Blank in order to study the effects of age and retirement on interest patterns. All subjects were of the Jewish faith and homo-

---

*The subjects had a mean age of 72 years and ranged in age from 62-83 years. The mean number of years retired was 7 and ranged from 1-27 years.

TABLE 5

CORRELATIONS OF SVIB GROUP SCORES WITH AGE
AND WITH NUMBER OF YEARS RETIRED

| Occupational Interest Grouping | Age | | No. Years Retired | |
|---|---|---|---|---|
| | r | P | r | P |
| I. Biological sciences | —.06 | — | .05 | — |
| II. Engineer & physical science | —.31 | — | —.17 | — |
| III. Production manager | .39 | <.05 | .20 | — |
| IV. Technical and/or skilled trades | .42 | <.01 | .39 | <.05 |
| V. Social services or welfare | .53 | <.01 | .40 | <.05 |
| VI. Musician | .05 | — | .13 | — |
| VII. C. P. A. | —.05 | — | —.19 | — |
| VIII. Business detail-administration | .49 | <.01 | .25 | — |
| IX. Sales or business contact | —.05 | — | —.22 | — |
| X. Verbal or linguistic | —.52 | <.01 | —.41 | <.01 |
| XI. President manu-facturing concern | —.29 | — | —.35 | <.05 |

geneous with respect to country of origin, work experience, and educational background. The younger retirants, compared to the older retirants, expressed strong interest in solitary activities involving greater independence, prestige, and material gain. The older retirants showed stronger interest in social interactional activities and ones which involve supervisory responsibilities of a somewhat lower status level (Tables 5 and 6). Thus, the degree and kind of change in interest patterns depend upon educational and socio-economic level. Among less educated and less wealthy older people, involving years of retirement and age appear to be associated with a stronger interest in social activities and social participation.

Kogan and Shelton (24) did an interesting study on attitudes and values of older and younger subjects. One question in this study was: "One of the greatest fears of many older people is _____." The older subjects mentioned death or dying while the younger ones mentioned lack of money and financial insecurity.

Bekker and Taylor (1966) used a questionnaire devised by Tuckman and Lorge which investigated the attitudes of both young and old people toward old age; the questionnaire contained items which they considered negative stereotypes and common misconceptions of old people. One hundred male and female undergraduates were asked to respond to the questionnaire for a kind of "average grandparent." The information enabled the authors to select students who came from four generation families and match them for age and sex with 50 students from three generation families. The responses of the 2 groups were found to differ primarily on 4 stereotype factors: personality traits, mental deterioration, physical characteristics and insecurity. Students of the 4 generation group attributed fewer negative characteristics to grandparents, perceiving them as having fewer characteristics of "old age." Twenty-year-olds with living grandparents saw their grandparents as less elderly than 20 year olds without living grandparents, although the grandparents were the same age in each group.

Cameron (1969) investigated perceived age stages by testing a random sample of 571 people aged 14-100, males and females, blacks and whites. He asked the following question: "What age do you think of when you hear or use "young adults"? He found that the adult life span was divided into four parts: "young adulthood" was between 18 and 25; there was then a gap until 40; "middle age" was between 40-55; this was followed by a 10 year gap. Finally old age was considered 65-80. After that people were considered "aged."

It is interesting that in two studies, those of Jyrkila (1960) and Busse et al (1967) indicate that old people who viewed themselves as old tend to be more maladjusted or sicker than those who viewed themselves as young, thus in the aged an accurate perception of one's own age does not seem indicative of a good adaptation.

Older people are greatly concerned with whether or not they are rejected or accepted by younger persons, but the reverse is not necessarily so. The attitude of an aged person toward other "old people" may be quite different from his attitudes toward *himself* in growing old. Studies also seem to indicate that the personal circumstances (primarily financial) of people over 60 tend to be

TABLE 6
COMPARISON OF YOUNGER AND OLDER SS
ON OCCUPATIONAL GROUPINGS

| Occupational Interest Grouping | Younger (N=16) | | Sample Older (N=23)* | | t | P |
|---|---|---|---|---|---|---|
| | Mean | S.D. | Mean | S.D. | | |
| I. Biological sciences | 22.7 | 6.05 | 22.1 | 4.75 | .35 | — |
| II. Engineer & physical science | 19.8 | 9.96 | 16.6 | 5.62 | 1.14 | — |
| III. Production manager | 32.5 | 7.56 | 37.7 | 7.20 | 2.18 | <.05 |
| IV. Technical and/or skilled trades | 19.5 | 11.30 | 27.1 | 9.26 | 2.32 | <.05 |
| V. Social services or welfare | 16.5 | 15.01 | 33.1 | 14.24 | 3.51 | <.01 |
| VI. Musician | 31.8 | 8.69 | 31.7 | 7.29 | .03 | — |
| VII. C. P. A. | 24.1 | 6.97 | 27.3 | 7.69 | 1.32 | — |
| VIII. Business detail-administration | 29.5 | 8.18 | 36.1 | 6.87 | 2.74 | <.01 |
| IX. Sales or business contact | 39.8 | 7.71 | 37.4 | 7.95 | .92 | — |
| X. Verbal or linguistic | 37.8 | 9.81 | 29.3 | 7.14 | 3.16 | <.01 |
| XI. President manu-facturing concern | 43.1 | 9.97 | 36.1 | 11.80 | 1.95 | .10 —.05 |

*Note—Younger group range in age from 62-69 years with a mean of 67 years. Older group range from 70-83 years with a mean of 74 years.

more important in determining attitudes and level of functioning than does chronological age.

Rosenfelt (25) has introduced the term "The Elderly Mystique" similar to the popular "Feminine Mystique" which refers to the ideas and attitudes held by an "in group," in this case the aged, toward old age. A subculture of the aging is being formed "arising from contempt for the inefficacy of the old which brings about rejection by the young and finally a mutual closing of ranks." As of this writing, we are still in the exploratory phase of investigating the ideas of this subculture about such topics as family and interpersonal relations, attitudes toward work and leisure, specific relationships among family members, and other vital issues in the areas of values of the aged.*

---

*See pages 157-159 for the attitude of the aged toward church and politics.

## WORK, PSYCHOLOGICAL TESTS AND COUNSELING WITH OLDER PEOPLE

A study by Le Gros Clark and Dunne (26) analyzed the employment of older people since 1921. The census data of 1921, 1931, and 1951 were used (no figures were available in 1941). Thirty-two occupations were examined from the point of view of determining the numbers of workers physically able to continue in their various occupations beyond their mid-sixties. The occupations selected were heavy labor (coal face workers), active jobs such as those of bus conductors, and sedentary work such as shop assistants and craftsmen — watchmakers, workers in precious metals, and makers of musical instruments. The authors defined the "survival rate" as "the proportion of the men who reached their mid-sixties in a given job and are physically capable of remaining on the same job into their late 60's or even in some cases beyond."

In 1956, the Bureau of Employment Security of the U. S. Department of Labor made a study of job orders placed with local employment service officers of the public employment services in seven different cities in different parts of the country. They found out that of some 21,000 job openings, 52% were restricted to those under 55, 30% to those under 45, and 10% to those under 30. A study in 1964 in 5 different cities involving over 500 establishments which together employ half a million workers indicated that only 6% of all new hirings during the year consisted of workers 45 years or older.

### Performance and Productivity

Although most studies show that the capacities of older workers do decline, because of the increased experience of older workers it does happen that capacity does improve. The results will vary somewhat with the kind of job and there is a continuous adjustment between the capacities of older workers and the requirements of their vocation. In contrast to office workers, men and women workers in footwear and furniture plants over the age of 55 show a tendency to decline in output. However, age changes are really of minor importance and placement depends on a knowledge of the capacities of the individual in relation to the requirements of each task. Individual differences even among older workers are great and many older workers are superior to the average young worker. One of the primary tasks of industry is to match changing workers to changing jobs. In order to do this, employers must know the specific demands of the job and the physical capacities of the employee. The older method of matching men and jobs is the intuitive one where men are matched to jobs according to the intuition of the boss. The planned methods are the disability method and the rating method. The disability method is based on the theory that jobs can be listed that are suitable for people with specific disabilities (e.g., one-armed, one-legged, arthritic, etc). The fallacy in this method is that is ignores the other abilities and capacities of the person. For example, in many industrial plants where jobs are set up for the "elderly," the stereotype infirmity is preserved and the abilities of the individual ignored. The rating method estimates surviving abilities on a rating basis and matches them with the job analysis. The problem here is that raters, while trying to be objective, are in reality subjective, and the language used by raters to describe both job demands and physical capacities is often not precise.

The Bureau of Employment Security of the U. S. Department of Labor analyzed the physical demands of 4000 jobs representative of industry in 1956 and it was found that only 14% of them — fewer than 600 out of the total 4000 — required any particular degree of physical strength or heavy lifting. With increasing automation this percentage will decrease, so that the complaint of many employers that older people cannot meet the company's physical requirements indicates there is something wrong with the requirements rather than the older workers.

There are many complications surrounding the productivity of workers with age. There is, for example, an early turnover in employees as young workers try different jobs and as industry encourages those it wishes to hold for longer employment.

Reemployment of the older worker is also a problem. Older workers have seniority, tend to devote less time in training for new kinds of jobs, and industry is less willing to train older workers. Finally, older workers may have "dated" kinds of jobs where the products themselves are distributed to the older segment of the population, and any expansion of the plant or change in the consumer habits may bring unemployment to the older worker.

## Accidents

One of the reasons for the reluctance of employers to hire older workers is that employers say they are "accident prone." However, many studies show the reverse is true. Speakman (27) listed 10 studies with 17 samples and 6 showed a rise in accident frequency with age, 9 showed a fall, and 2 undetermined. Both Kossoris (28) and Vernon (29) showed that accident rates were highest among the younger workers. Similar findings were revealed in studies by the New York Joint Legislative Committee on Unemployment, the Wisconsin Industrial Commission, and the International Labor Office.

## PSYCHOLOGICAL TESTING

The use of psychological tests with older people has been discussed previously.* In general, those psychological tests which can be used with adults can be used with people beyond the age of 65. However, counselors should try to assess each individual older person on such tests with regard to motivation, sensory and perceptual acuity, and physical condition of the testee. Since tests of selection are used quite extensively in industry, Odell (30) reports that older workers are at a disadvantage when tested against standards which have been evolved from groups other than the aged. He also reports on a cross sectional analysis by year-age groups of the 400-case general population sample in which the GATB was standardized. All of the abilities measured declined with age with the rate of decline varying with different aptitudes. In general, test results for G (General Intelligence), V (Verbal facility), N (Numerical Ability), and S (Space Perception) seem least affected by age. The tests results for Q (clerical ability), and P (form perception) show a moderate decline with age by age

*See pp. 45-47, supra.

groups. The test results for A (aiming), T (tapping), F (finger dexterity) and M (Manual dexterity) show the sharpest and steepest decline.

A word should be said here about some of the newer findings concerning the use of projective testing with older people. As with other tests, the main handicaps in using present projective diagnostic techniques is the lack of reliable norms for older age groups. As of this writing, the only large scale study of the responses of the elderly to a projective test is that of the Rorschach (31), although there have been studies investigating the reliability and validity of diagnostic tests with the older population in general, uncovering their special significance for this age group (32). The Bender-Gestalt has been found to be a fairly reliable test for identifying brain damage in older people. Fifteen signs have been developed by Hain (33) to diagnose diffuse cortical damage resulting from cerebro-vascular disease. The Bender-Gestalt combined with the Draw A Person are predictive when terminal planning is necessary. Changes in size and accuracy of the drawings are correlated with illness and death. The Holtzman Ink Blot Technique is useful because of its isolation of variables which are important in the older age groups such as hostility, anxiety, reality testing and impulse control. In the Holtzman, rejection of inkblot cards are important. Constriction, reaction time, and popular responses are all important diagnostic signs in the elderly on both the Rorschach and the Holtzman. There have been several attempts to develop specific projective tests for the aging. The Gerontological Apperception Test (34) patterned after the TAT consists of 13 cards depicting situations typifying various problems and conflict areas considered to be common in aging.

Verbal learning tasks are satisfactory for further separating organic and functional tasks. Inglis (1970) designed the New

---

*A test quite useful in industry, with older people, because of its non-verbal nature and ease of taking and extensive norms is one devised by the author. The Geist Picture Interest Inventory published by Western Psychological Services, 12031 Wilshire Blvd., Los Angeles, California, 90025. A modification of this test used in industry with deaf people is the Geist Picture Interest Inventory: Deaf Edition, published by the same publishers.

World Word Learning and Retention Test and it is well standardized among older groups. The Paired Associate Learning Test and the Modified Word Learning Test do an adequate job in separating organics, functionals and normals while the Synonym Learning Test seems to have a high correlation with psychiatric diagnosis in the elderly. The Digit Copying Test (Clement 1963) discriminates between organic and depressive states. Despite the assertions of some people, the "hold"—"don't hold" subtests of the WAIS do not seem to "work" in predicting intellectual deterioration in the aged.

As with other kinds of tests, the person doing the testing must use certain special precautions. Such elements as the physical, psychosocial anxiety factors and motivation must be taken into account. As stated previously,* tests become more threatening generally with the aged and performance is more likely to be affected by non-test factors all of which must be considered in interpreting test results. In the evaluation of projective tests, the important element with the aging, much more so than with other groups, is the clinician's attentiveness and knowldege of the aging process itself.

The psychologist who uses any single test with older people as the only measure of function and personality must guard against overinterpretation. This is particularly true with the Bender-Gestalt, since the brain damaged older person has a reservoir of stored memory and information as well as a variety of adjustive habits developed over a lifetime which may be mobilized for his rehabilitation. With the passage of time, there will undoubtedly be many and varied purposes for diagnostic testing with the aged such as planning for retirement and pre-retirement counseling, counseling in family and marital situations, future planning for living arrangements, post-retirement careers and perhaps even assessment for candidacy for psychotherapy.

## SENSORY AND PERCEPTUAL PROCESSES

### Sensory Processes

One of the most important functions of any organism is its ability to interact with its internal and external environment.

*See p 45

The ability to interact will depend on how much information the organism can get about the environment and this will depend upon the reception of information from sensory receptors located at specialized nerve endings in the eye, ear, skin, and muscles. Neurophysiologists divide neural mechanisms into "sensory" and "perceptual." The human organism has a built-in apparatus whereby there are large safety margins. There is more sensory input than is necessary for the detection or discrimination of signals. In addition, information from other sense organs can be used to increase adaptation. The consequence to the individual of reduced sensory acuity depends upon how critical the sensory system is to his everyday life. For example, visual acuity would be much more important to a bus driver than a minister. Certain terms should be defined.

1) *Sensory Acuity, Sensation, Sensory Processes.* These terms, almost synonymous, refer to the ability to be aware of simple stimuli, like touch, taste, odor, vibration, noise, light and dark. When these stimuli become more complex, they are called perceptions. Perception indicates interpretation or meaning while sensory acuity refers to awareness.

2) *Threshold.* The magnitude of the stimulus which is just at the level of awareness, or the stimulus of the smallest magnitude that produces a sensation.

3) *Absolute Threshold.* The lowest magnitude of a stimulus that can be perceived.

4) *Difference Threshold.* When there is a difference in the change of environments, the difference threshold is defined as the increment in the magnitude of the stimulus necessary for the difference to be perceived. As people get older, there is a reduction in sensory acuity as a result of injury, disease, and changes in the structure and function of nervous tissue.

**Vision**

Visual functions have been studied rather extensively, but very few have been studied in relation to age. The primary measurement that reflects the efficacy of vision is the measurement of visual acuity. Visual acuity is the smallest object that the subject can perceive. It is usually expressed as the ratio of the distance between the visual object and the subject over the distance the normal eye can discriminate the same details, or the visual angle subtended by the smallest object that the subject can perceive. In the testing of visual acuity, letters of the alphabet are used as the test object. The distance at which a subject can see letters of a given size, usually seen by persons with normal vision at 20 feet, expresses his visual acuity. Visual acuity is poor in children but improves up to young adulthood; from 25-50 there is a decline in visual acuity and for many persons there is a decline thereafter. The size of the pupil tends to decrease with age. Howell (35), in a neurological examination of 200 healthy patients ranging from 65-91 years, found reaction of both pupils to light in 54% of the cases, in one eye in only 9% and no response to light in either eye in 37%. Thus, the incidence of positive reaction to light tends to decrease with age. An older person's vision will improve relatively more than a younger person's when the general illumination is raised.

The performance of the older subjects is markedly better than younger when the illumination is raised. At the higher levels of illumination, the performance of older subjects draws closer to younger, but at no level of illumination does acuity of the older subject reach that of younger ones.

### Accommodation

The eye focuses on objects at various distances by changing the focal length of the lens. At rest, the normal eye will focus objects which are at an infinite distance. The eye accommodates to focus on new objects by shortening the focal distance of its lens. Older subjects have a more fixed focus with less ability to adjust to objects close to the eye. As we get older there is a decrease in accommodation to light.

### Dark Adaptation

Dark adaptation is the phenomenon wherein there is an increase in visual sensitivity after remaining in the dark. It has been repeatedly demonstrated that the dark-adaptation threshold increases with age. There appears to be a slight drop in the threshold up to the second decade and then a gradual acceleration. The rise is very marked past the sixth decade. In general, the rate of adaptation or the change in threshold as a function of time in the dark is not closely related to age but the light threshold itself is related to age. Thus, older persons will have difficulty driving an automobile in the dark since it will take a longer time for an older person's eyes to recover their sensitivity after passing a car with oncoming bright lights than a younger person and bright lights seriously impede an older person's length of non-seeing.* In a study by Guth *et al.* on the lighting requirements of older workers, each subject whose eyes were corrected for refractive errors attempted to read 10 seven letter words under different conditions of illumination. Figures 9a-9g show that as one gets older, he needs greater illumination to obtain equal visual recognition.** Older people in general benefit more by increasing environmental illumination.

**Critical Flicker Fusion**

Critical Flicker Fusion (CFF) is the ability of a subject to perceive a flashing light as a fused and glowing source. CFF does decline with age, that is the number of cycles per second increases with older subjects. Experimenters have ascertained that the pupil of the older subject does get smaller as the person grows older and this limits the amount of light entering the eye.

*A project by the Duke University on Longitudinal Study of Aging, sheds light on this whole subject of driving. As part of a Social Worker's interview, a panel of elderly participants was asked:

    (1) Whether he learned to drive. (2) Whether he was continuing to drive. (3) What limitations or restrictions were placed on his driving, voluntary or otherwise. (4) If he had stopped driving, and if so why?

The results indicate that older drivers do have accidents at a higher rate than younger adults, and their accidents frequency experience per miles driven compared with that of adolescent drivers is relatively lower. However, because of their avoidance of lengthy driving situations and the usually fewer miles driven per year, the percentage of all accidents as compared to percentages of drivers in this group is lower than adolescence. The driving accidents of the elderly are usually caused by errors of omission rather than commission eg. incorrect turning or failing to keep a proper look-out, rather than speeding or tailgaiting, characteristic of adolescence. Very few older people drink while driving. Comparing the drivers with ex-drivers, the drivers are more happy and satisfied than the ex-drivers. The loss of mobility, status and increased dependence on others, makes it particularly difficult for elderly males to give up driving.

**The captions accompanying each graph are self explanatory and indicate the state of the eye under varying conditions with increasing age.

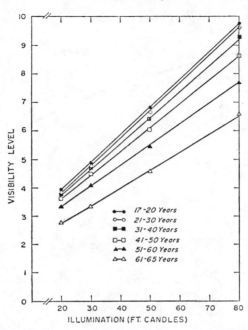

Figure 9. The relationship between illumination and visibility level for different age groups. (Adapted from Guth *et al.*, 1956.)

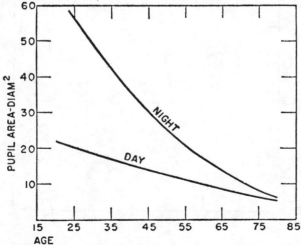

Figure 9a. Age reduces the amount of pupil area available for seeing. It reduces the night-time area more sharply than the day-time. This information is from the *Illuminating Engineering Society Lighting handbook.*

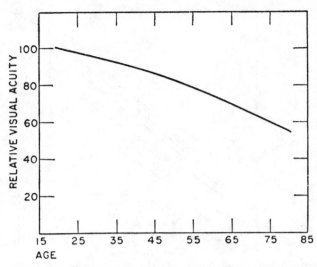

Figure 9b. Visual acuity is reduced by approximately 50 per cent between the ages 20 and 80. This graph is also based on figures from the *IES Lighting Handbook*.

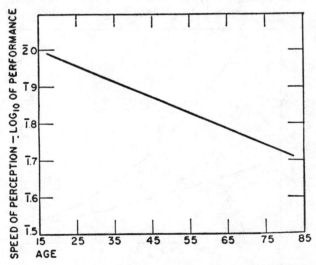

Figure 9c. This is a line presentation of how the speed of perception is reduced as the age of the eye is increased. It is based on findings by H. C. Weston, *British Journal of Ophtalmology*, Sept., 1948.

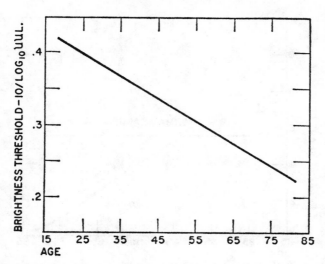

Figure 9d. In moving from a bright to a dark area, the ability to see is sharply reduced with age. This graph is based on statements by McFarland, Domey, Warren and Ward in *Highway Research Board Bulletin 255*.

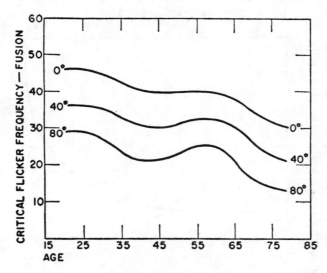

Figure 9e. The ability to perceive movement at various degrees off center of view is shown in undulating decline as age increases. The graph is based on Ernst Wolf's article, "Effects of Age on Peripheral Vision" in the *Highway Research Board Bulletin 336*.

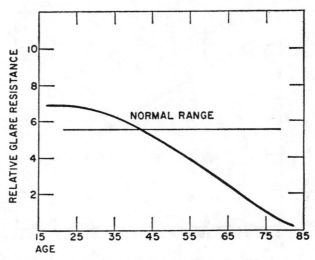

Figure 9f. This chart shows how much less able is the older eye to resist glare that washes out the visual image. Figures are from an article concerned with safety in automobiles, by E. D. Fletcher, "An Investigation of Glare Resistance and its Relationship to Age, published by the California State Division of Drivers' Licenses.

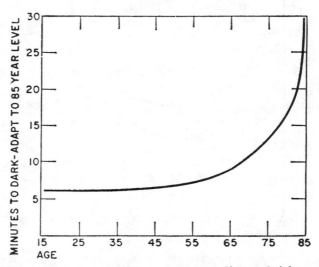

Figure 9g. Eyes of "young-normals" need time to adjust to brightness changes. Eyes aged 20 through 65 gradually need more. Eyes over 65 need a sharp increase. This information from the same source as Figure 9f.

## Color

There are some definite changes with age insofar as color vision is concerned. These are: At about the 6th decade there is a tendency of the lens to yellow which serves to diminish transmission of the wave lengths from green to violet, or the shorter wave lengths. There is also a reduction in the sensitivity of the retina or central structures to blue light and possibly to the green and red parts of the spectrum as well. These findings pose implications for the elderly who work with colors.

## Degenerative Changes

Practically all the tissues of the eye are subject to change with advancing age. They may exhibit themselves by alteration in function or by visible degenerative disturbances. In almost all individuals past the age of 40, ocular tissue will show senile alterations although they may only be in the initial stages. In a study by Belloc (37) in California, 85% of blindness had its onset after the age of 45, with half beginning after 65 and another 30% occurring between 45-64.

The most recent work on degeneration of vision with age has been done by Anderson (Banks, Jr.) and Palmore (Erdman) at the Duke University Center for the Study of Aging and Human Development, where ocular function was evaluated longitudinally and cross sectionally as well as correlated with longevity and social variables. In a cross sectional analysis, a best corrected vision of 20/50 or worse occurred in 8% of those aged 60-69, 14% of those 70-79 and 36% of those over 80. A longitudinal study found increases in this percentage of 13 points for the 60-69 group and a 32 point increase in the 70-79 group. The incidence of glaucoma increased longitudinally with age as did the incidence of cornea guttata. The incidence and increase in the number of cataracts was less in the longitudinal analysis, than in the cross sectional. Specific ocular conditions seem not generally related to impaired activity or attitudes unless they cause a substantial deterioration in the vision of both eyes.

## Audition

The prevalence of impaired hearing is quite marked at the upper age levels. Beasley showed that the average hearing loss showed a marked increase past the age of 45 and continued to increase rapidly thereafter. After the age of 55, there is a consistent sex difference. Males show a greater incidence and prevalence of hearing impairment than females. In general, individuals over 65 have difficulty in perceiving tones over 10,000 cycles/second. The reason for the sex difference past the age of 55 is not known, but it may be because men are exposed to higher noise levels in their occupations than women.

The reason for presbycusis* in both sexes may be damage or degeneration of the peripheral or central auditory mechanisms. Peripheral mechanisms are those due to impairment of the ear and auditory nerve while central mechanisms are those associated with perception which will be discussed later in this chapter.

One of the reasons for impaired hearing in the aged is an increase in the rigidity of the basilar membrane. In a rather extensive study which included clinical examinations, audiograms, and examinations of the pathology of the cochlea and middle ear, Crowe (38) *et al.* found a correspondence between high tone loss and pathology in the lower cochlea. Crowe described two types of loss—the "gradual" and "abrupt." Almost all the gradual showed primarily loss of nerve fibers without much change in the Organs of Corti. The "abrupt" group did show pathology in the Organ of Corti and nerve fiber loss. Studies by other investigators indicate that the primary pathology in the peripheral mechanism is the atrophy and disappearance of the ganglion cells with subsequent degeneration of the hair cells in the Organ of Corti. In studying hearing loss of the aged by measuring the voltage across the cochlea and nerves in the ear, it was found that there was a much larger decrease of voltage across the nerves as compared to the cochlea. This substantiates the previous findings of path-

---

*Decrease in hearing due to advancing age.

ology in examining the tissues of these organs under the microscope.

The most recent findings in the field of audition again have
been done in a 7 year follow-up study at the Duke Center for the
Study of Aging and Human Development by Eisdorfer (Carl) and
Wilkie (Frances). This study was a longitudinal one among the
same 92 individuals initially seen at ages 60-79 years. The
increasing magnitude of hearing loss across the seven year period
for the younger subjects who advanced in average age from 67-74
years was about the same as the older subjects averaging 75-82
years. Women had better hearing than men at the higher
frequencies. Blacks and particularly black men had superior
hearing to their white counterparts at the low as well as higher
frequencies. The authors believed that a large part of this
difference was due to previous exposure to noise.

Corso (1971) has suggested that research be directed toward the
investigation of functioning across various modalities to explore
neural coding, sensory input storage and intolerance of tests.
Greenberg has suggested that older people may have an
impairment in converting visual stimuli into auditory storage
and should benefit most in learning and retaining information by
techniques that facilitate auditory maintenance of the trace as it is
being processed, although this is not directly connected with
audition but the whole gamut of sensory modalities, such things
as differential susceptibility to certain illusions, a decreased
ability to abstract information to imbedded figures, difficulties in
handling irrelevant stimuli and changes in information processing and signal detection occurs in the older person.

**Taste and Smell**

The threshold of taste with advancing age is practically unknown. Bourliére *et al.* studied the effect of age on perception
and recognition thresholds for sugar and salt. For salty tastes, he
found that only the threshold of perception increased with age
and that only in men. The threshold of recognition in men was
higher than that in women at all ages. There is a definite change

in the gustatory apparatus, with a great reduction in the number of taste buds after the age of 70. There also is a decline in olfactory functions with age parallelled by an atrophy of the olfactory organs, just as with the taste organs.

## Touch

Touch sensitivity appears to be unchanged from an early adulthood through 50-55 with an increase in threshold after that age. There is a decrease in the number of areas responding to touch for all kinds of stimuli, which indicates either a decrease in the number of receptors or of their sensitivity with age.

## Pain and Temperature

Very few studies have been done on the sensitivity to pain and age, but in those that have been completed the results are contradictory. Clinically, it has been found that there is a decreased sensitivity to pain with increasing age, but experimentally this has not been found to be true. Likewise with temperature, it has been found clinically that there is a diminution of sensitivity to temperature with age, but there is no experimental data as of this writing to back this up. There are indications that the elderly are less able to maintain their normal body temperature when exposed to cold.

## PSYCHOMOTOR SKILLS

Psychomotor skills are those activities where there are both voluntary coordinated movements of the body or parts of the body and the capacity to execute these movements. It is well known that there is a slowing of such performance with age. However, it is not clear whether this retardation is due to the changes in the sense organs, whether central mechanisms are involved, or whether these changes are genetic and irreversible or due to trauma and disease which may be reversible and preventable.

One of the classic methods in measuring changes in psychomotor skills is reaction time. Reaction time is the period elapsing between the appearance of a signal and the beginning of a respondent movement. The results of studies of various kinds of reaction time and age are shown in Figure 10. One can see that reaction time does increase with age, but that this is relatively small and there is relatively little difference in the length of reaction in the separate sense modalities of vision and hearing.

The literature suggests that the changes in the nervous system leading to reduced reaction time in older people are not under the voluntary control of the individual. Usually such things as cell loss, slowing peripheral nerve conduction and changes in synaptic conduction have been suggested as the etiology in biological terms for the irreversible slowing of behavior. Biofeedback may be a useful tool in manipulating physiological parameters such as cortical excitability and nerve firing to find if slowing is indeed beyond adaptive control. Variability in individual differences in reaction time is more marked in older than younger people.

One of the basic skills is motor skills. Experiments indicate that until the 40's or 50's the time spent in making movements in response to signals to various motor skills do not rise or at least rise very little, but the decrease in performance occurs primarily during those portions of the motor task where the signals are being perceived and the responding actions prepared, i.e., during the reaction times. Other experiments suggest that the reason may be twofold: First, older people seem to be less able than younger to overlap the planning of one movement with the execution of a previous one; secondly, older people make movements with greater care and meticulousness than younger. This difference in reaction time, whatever its cause, is extremely important in accident proneness and prevention. Over half the total fatal accidents of people over 65 occur in the home. It may be that the reduction in reaction time of older people is due to physical changes since people liable to falls were judged to be less medically fit than those not liable to falls. (40) It is possible that people who maintain physical fitness will have better control over their movements than those who do not, and for those older people undergoing senescent pathological changes, a well designed physical environment is important to minimize risks.

## SIMPLE REACTION TIMES
### (IN SECONDS)

| Author | Type of Reaction† | Teens | Twenties | Thirties | Forties | Fifties | Sixties | Seventies | Eighties | Notes |
|---|---|---|---|---|---|---|---|---|---|---|
| Galton (1899); see also Koga and Morant (1923) | Press key in response to sound | 0.187 | 0.182 | 0.181 | 0.190 | 0.186 | 0.206 | 0.205 | ...... | Subjects were visitors to an international health exhibition. The figures have been calculated approximately from those given by Koga and Morant. |
| | Release key in response to sound | .158 | .154 | .158 | .159 | .157 | .167 | .174 | ...... | |
| Miles (1931a) | Press key in response to light | ...... | .23 | .24 | .22 | .20 | .28 | .30 | .28 | 100 subjects: fewer in the twenties and eighties than other ranges. The twenties ranged from 25 to 29 only. |
| | Press key in response to sound | ...... | .21 | .22 | .22 | .22 | .23 | .26 | .28 | |
| | Lift foot in response to sound | ...... | .22 | .22 | .24 | .24 | .26 | .27 | .30 | |
| Bellis (1933) | Press key in response to light Men | .24 | .22 | .26 | .27 | .38 | ...... | ...... | ...... | 20 subjects in each age range except the highest which had 10. Equal numbers of men and women in each range. Scores are means of best five readings by each subject. |
| | Women | .32 | .26 | .34 | .36 | .44 | ...... | ...... | ...... | |
| | Press key in response to sound in headphones Men | .23 | .19 | .24 | .25 | .37 | ...... | ...... | ...... | |
| | Women | .31 | .20 | .30 | .30 | .42 | ...... | ...... | ...... | |
| DeSilva (1936) | "Brake reaction time" in a test designed to simulate car driving (subject raised foot from accelerator pedal and transferred it to brake on seeing red flash of a traffic light) | .418 | .418 | .428 | .442 | .455 | .465 | ...... | ...... | 2000 subjects. The age range of the teens is 16-19 and of the sixties, 61-65. The figures are approximately only, having been taken from a graph included in De Silva's paper. |
| Ficandt et al. (1956) | Pressing button in response to light | 0.228 | .201 | .201 | .217 | .212 | .217 | .245 | 0.353 | The age ranges were 11-14, 21-24, 29-36, 39-47, 49-56, 59-67, 69-79, and 80-88. Each of the 120 subjects gave five readings. The two extremes of these were excluded and the scores were the means of the remaining three. |
| Cesa-Bianchi (1955) | Response to light | ...... | .215 | .186 | .202 | .207 | .214 | ...... | ...... | 268 subjects mostly between 30 and 59. The oldest age range was 60-66. Very full scores given for individual subjects. |
| | Response to sound | ...... | .157 | .161 | .179 | .167 | .187 | ...... | ...... | |

†All are made with the hand unless otherwise stated.

Figure 10.

The importance of the whole problem of psychomotor skills in general and reaction time in particular to the aging process is evidenced in the transportation industry. Airline pilots, truck drivers, bus drivers and drivers of vehicles in general should have the interest of the public at large. It is well known that older pilots and public vehicle drivers have excellent records insofar as safety is concerned, but companies must figure in long-term probabilty ranges. Pacaud (41) reports an experiment on 4000 operatives and apprentices on the French railways. The subjects were told to:

1. Raise the right foot on seeing a green light.
2. Press the right foot on seeing a red light.
3. Make both movements on seeing a yellow light.

After the tasks had been learned, it was further complicated by the requirement that when a light signal was given by a sound of metallic quality, a key was to be pressed and the usual reaction to the light omitted. Success on the performance of these tasks fell steadily from the early twenties on to the end of the age scale. The decrease seems to be much less when the respondents were required to light the signals alone and the sound signals omitted. Such tasks are components of many commercial pilots' and drivers' examinations and have wide implications for safety. There are, no doubt, wide individual differences and thus frequent medical examinations of older operatives by commercial companies who employ drivers is indicated. The number of older automobile drivers (65 and over) is increasing relative to the increase of older people in the United States. Figure 11 shows the involvement rate by sex and age of passenger car drivers during the night and day. Strangely enough, except for male night drivers, the driver above 70 is more likely to have a highway accident than those between 16-20, the latter group having been the topic of a great deal of controversial debate.

## TRACKING PERFORMANCE

"Tracking" or following a moving target changes a great deal with age, being more pronounced at high speeds, i.e., when the

targent is moving at high speeds. In an experiment by Welford
(41), he had subjects keep a pointer which they could move by
means of a handle in line with a target moved back and forth
by a cam. In two additional experiments, the subject was asked
to "drive" a ballpoint pen along a track on a paper drawn past
a window. The control was a steering wheel and the apparatus ar-

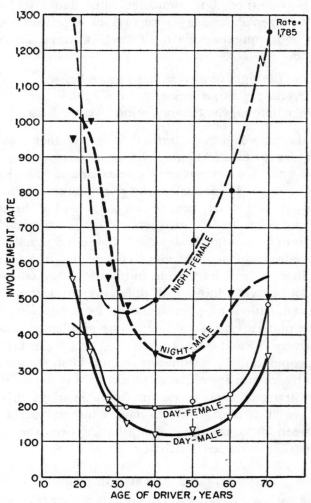

Figure 11. Involvement rate by sex and age of passenger-car driver, day and
night.

ranged in such a manner that more or less of the track could be seen ahead of the pen.

The results showed that at low speeds subjects could track fairly well in step with the target but as the speed increased, tracking became more difficult and this difficulty increased with age.

## ORGANIZATION OF COMPLEX PERFORMANCE

It has been mentioned previously that the physical performance of older people is impaired by a variety of factors—the difficulty of overlapping, the organization of one action with the execution of a previous action and the irregularity of timing of older people. Inaccuracy of performance of older people is compensated for by them taking more time and looking more closely and more continuously at what they are doing. (42)

These compensations seem to enable the aged to weld their action into larger units much like the younger and thus organization of performance by older persons does not seem to be impaired by age.

## INDUSTRIAL OPERATIONS AND OCCUPATIONAL SKILLS

There have been a number of studies which indicate proficiency of both occupational and industrial skills with age. Heavy work in general is commonly regarded as not suitable for the elderly. Richardson (43) and Le Gros Clark (44) have shown fairly conclusively that in the later years there is a trend for men to engage in lighter work than in their earlier years. Richardson, in a study on coal miners found that this trend toward lighter work was due to not so much the physical demands of the job, but the work could be done at the men's own pace. Both speed and physical effort enter into the definition of work suitable for older people but it is speed which limits them. In industry, there is a trend to employ younger men where speed is required. Those jobs where speed is not an important factor are changed in the early 50's while the change to less strenuous work occurs in the 60's. There are many intrinsic factors which affect the effective performance of older workers. It is well known, for example, that industrial efficiency does decrease with age, but older people tend to take care of their aging handicaps more than younger people take care of their deficiencies, and it is possible that an older employed worker with a hearing aid and glasses may be more effective than a younger one without such accoutrements. As a matter of fact, considering total job behavior, the older worker is found to be more efficient in comparison with the younger, particularly if such characteristics as accuracy, absenteeism, and motivation are taken into account.

## ATHLETIC SKILLS

Table 7 shows the ages at which individuals have exhibited peak athletic proficiency. There are many factors which go into the components of an individual athletic skill, viz., endurance, strength, precision, reaction time, and various kinds of responses, and their component will vary with the skill and age. For example, boxing champions will tend to be younger than golf champions because the component skills of golf requires less and different demands on the athlete than those of boxing.

## ACCIDENTS

King and Speakman (45), in a study, show that industrial accidents tend to occur according to circumstances, and that in some cases the frequency of accidents falls with age and in others, rises. The accidents that are sustained by older people tend to be due to the slowness in appreciating the hazards or taking action to avoid them. Whitfield (46) found in a study of coal miners that younger accident prone men tended to perform poorly on perceptual, memory, or cognitive tests and do well on tracking performance while the older men do well on perceptual and cognitive tests but poorly at tracking. Table 8, which shows the number of disabling injuries per 500 workers, indicates that the group over 65 is among the lowest of all workers which may be a reflection of slowness and carefulness among older people. Perhaps a modification of design of jobs to lessen the requirements for rapid action or the risks of sudden hazards could bring many jobs now confined to the young, to within the reach of the old.

## TABLE 7
### AGES AT WHICH INDIVIDUALS HAVE EXHIBITED PEAK PROFICIENCY AT "PHYSICAL" SKILLS

| Type of Skill | Number of Cases | Median Age | Mean Age | Years of Maximum Proficiency |
|---|---|---|---|---|
| U.S.A. outdoor tennis champions .............. | 89 | 26.35 | 27.12 | 22-26 |
| Runs batted in: annual champions of the two major baseball leagues ...... | 49 | 27.10 | 27.97 | 25-29 |
| U.S.A. indoor tennis champions .............. | 64 | 28.00 | 27.45 | 25-29 |
| World champion heavyweight pugilists ........ | 77 | 29.19 | 29.51 | 26-30 |
| Base stealers: annual champions of the two major baseball leagues ....... | 31 | 29.21 | 28.85 | 26-30 |
| Indianapolis Speedway racers and national auto-racing champions ........ | 82 | 29.56 | 30.18 | 27-30 |
| Best hitters: annual champions of the two major baseball leagues ........ | 53 | 29.70 | 29.56 | 27-31 |
| Best pitchers: annual champions of the two major baseball leagues ....... | 51 | 30.10 | 30.03 | 28-32 |
| Open golf champions of England and of the U.S.A. ..... | 127 | 30.72 | 31.29 | 28-32 |
| National individual rifle-shooting champions ....... | 84 | 31.33 | 31.45 | 32-34 |
| State corn-husking champions of the U.S.A. ........ | 103 | 31.50 | 30.66 | 28-31 |
| World, national, and state pistol-shooting champions .......... | 47 | 31.90 | 30.63 | 31-34 |
| National amateur bowling champions .......... | 58 | 32.33 | 32.78 | 30-34 |
| National amateur duck-pin bowling champions ..... | 91 | 32.35 | 32.19 | 30-34 |
| Professional golf champions of England and the U.S.A. ..... | 53 | 32.44 | 32.14 | 29-33 |
| World record-breakers at billiards ........ | 42 | 35.00 | 35.67 | 30-34 |
| World champion billiardists ......... | 74 | 35.75 | 34.38 | 31-35 |

*Source:* H. C. Lehman: *Age and Achievement.* Princeton, Princeton University Press, 1953, p. 256.

TABLE 8
INJURY EXPERIENCE BY AGE OF WORKER

| Age Group | Injury Frequency Disabling | | | Injury Severity (Disability) | |
|---|---|---|---|---|---|
| | Per Million Man Hours | Per 500 Workers | Nondisabling Per Million Man Hours | Average Days' Disability | Average Days' Healing |
| 15-24 .......... | 6.6 | 5.9 | 1328 | 20.2 | 29.5 |
| 25-34 .......... | 9.1 | 8.8 | 1475 | 9.2 | 29.0 |
| 35-44 .......... | 11.9 | 9.2 | 1145 | 12.7 | 31.3 |
| 45-54 .......... | 8.7 | 8.8 | 855 | 17.7 | 37.0 |
| 55-64 .......... | 9.9 | 9.0 | 604 | 18.0 | 40.8 |
| 65 and over .... | 8.3 | 7.2 | 408 | 12.9 | 49.0 |

*Source:* R. A. McFarland and B. O'Doherty, Work and Occupational Skills. In J. E. Birren (ed.), *Handbook of Aging and the Individual* (Chicago: University of Chicago Press, 1959), p. 469.

# BIBLIOGRAPHY

1. Zubek, J. P., and Friend, Celia M.: The effects of age on critical thinking ability. *J. Gerontology, 13:*410, 1958.

2. Jerome, E. A.: Decay of heuristic process in the aged. In: Tibbitts, C., and Donohue, Wilma, (eds.) : *Aging Around the World.* Columbia University Press, New York City, pp. 808-823, 1962.

3. Foster, J. C., and Taylor, G. A.: The applicability of mental tests to persons over fifty years of age. *J. Applied Psychol., 4:*39-58, 1920.

4. Beeson, M. F.: Intelligence at senescence. *J. Applied Psychol., 4:*219-234, 1920.

5. Yerkes, R. M.: Psychological Examining in the United States Army. National Academy of Science, Washington, D. C., U. S. Government Printing Office, 1921.

6. Bilash, I., and Zubek, J. P.: The effects of age on factorially "pure" mental abilities. *J. Gerontol., 15:*175-182, 1960.

7. Willoughby, G. R.: Family Similarities in Mental Test Abilities. Genetic Psychol. Monographs, 2:235-277, 1927.

8. Corsini, R. J., and Fassett, K. K.: Intelligence and aging. *J. Genet Psychol., 82:*249-264, 1953.

9. Riegel, K. F.: Ergebnisse und Probleme der Psychologischen Alternforschung. *Vita Humana, 1:*52-64, 1958.

10. Miles, Catherine C.: The influence of speed and age on intelligence test scores in adults. *J. Gen. Psychol., 10:*208-210, 1934.

11. Kaplan, O. J.: Intellectual changes of normal senescence. In: Stieglitz, E. S. (ed.) : *Geriatric Medicine,* 3rd Ed. Philadelphia, J. B. Lippincott Co., 1954, pp. 82-91.

12. Dennis, W.: Age and productivity among scientists. *Science, 123:*724-25, 1956.
13. Kurihara, H.: General intelligence test and its norm. I. Standardization of intelligence tests for children, adolescents and adults. II. Mental development of the Japanese. *Rep. Inst. Sc. Labor, Japan, 25:*1-22, 1934.
14. Stone, C. P.: The age factor in animal learning. *Genetic Psychol.* Monographs, 1929, No. 5, pp. 1-30, No. 6, pp. 125-202.
15. Birren, J. E.: Age differences in learning in a two choice water maze by rats. *J. Gerontology, 17:*207-213, 1962.
16. Verzár-McDougall, E. J.: Studies in learning and memory in aging rats. *Gerontologia, 1:*65-85, 1957.
17. Gladis, M., and Braun, H. W.: Age differences in transfer and retroaction as a function of intertask similarity. *J. Exp. Psychol., 55:*25-30, 1958.
18. Ruch, F. L.: The differentiative effect of age upon learning. *J. Genetic Psychol., 11:*261-286, 1934.
19. U. S. Department of Labor, Industrial Retraining Programs for Technological Change. Washington, D. C., U. S. Government Printing Office, Bureau of Labor Statistics, Bull. No. 1368, 1963, pp. 10-12.
20. U. S. Department of Labor, Industrial Retraining Programs for Technological Change. Washington, D. C., U. S. Government Printing Office, Bureau of Labor Statistics, Bull. No. 1368, 1963, pp. 28-29.
21. Belbin, Eunice: Methods of training older workers. *Ergonomics, 1:*207-221, 1958.
22. Kogan, N., and Wallach, M. A.: Age changes in values and attitudes. *J. Gerontology, 16:*272-280, 1961.
23. Cameron, Paul: Masculinity-femininity in the aged. *J. Gerontology, 23:* 1, 63-70, Jan. 1968.
24. Kogan, N., and Shelton, Florence C.: Beliefs about old people: A comparative study of older and younger samples. *J. Genetic Psychol., 100:* 93-111, 1962.
25. Rosenfelt, Rosalie H.: The elderly mystique in old age as a social issue. *J. Social Issues., XXI:*No. 4, 37, October, 1965.
26. Le Gros Clark, F., and Dunne, A. C.: *Ageing in Industry.* New York, Philosophical Library, 1965.
27. Speakman, D.: Bibliography of Research on Changes in Work Capacity With Age. London, Ministry of Labor and National Service. National Advisory Committee on the Employment of Older Men and Women, 1956.
28. Kossoris, M. D.: Relation of age to industrial injuries. *Monthly Labor Rev., 51* (4) *:*789-804, 1940.
29. Vernon, H. M.: *Accidents and Their Prevention.* Cambridge, Mass., Cambridge University Press, 1936.
30. Odell, C. E.: Aptitudes and work performance of the older workers. In:

Anderson, J. E. (ed.) : *Psychological Aspects of Aging.* Washington, D. C., American Psychological Association, 1956, pp. 240-244.

31. Ames, Louise B., Learned, Janet, Metraux, Ruth W., and Walker, R. N.: *Rorschach Responses in Old Age.* New York, Hoeber-Harper, 1954.

32. Oberleider, Muriel: Aging — Its importance for clinical psychology. In: Abt, L. E., and Riess, B. F. (ed.) : *Progress in Clinical Psychology.* New York, Grunne and Stratton, 1964, pp. 158-171.

33. Hain, J. D.: The Bender Gestalt Test: A scoring method for identifying brain damage. *J. Consulting Psychol., 28:*34-40, 1964.

34. Walk, R. L., Rustin, S. L., and Seiden, Rochelle: A projective technique for the aged. *J. Long Island Consultation Center, 4:*7-17, 1966.

35. Howell, T. H.: Senile deterioration in the central nervous system. *Brit. Med. J., II:*No. 4592, 56-58, 1949.

36. Guth, S. K., Eastman, A. A., and McNelis, J. F.: Lighting requirements for older workers. *Illuminating Engineering, 51:*656-660, 1956.

37. Belloc, Nedra: Blindness among the aged. *Public Health Reports, 71:* 1221-1255, 1956.

38. Crowe, S. J., Guild, S. A., and Polvogt, L. M.: Observations on the pathology of high tone deafness. John Hopkins Hospital, *54:*315-379, 1934.

39. Bourliére, F., Cendron, H., and Rappaport, A.: Modification avec l'âge des seúils gustatifs de perception et de reconnaissance aux saveurs saleé et sucrée chez l'homme. *Gerontologia, 2:*104-112, 1958.

40. Droller, H.: Falls and accidents in a random sample of elderly people living at home. *Geriatrics, 10:*239-244, 1955.

41. Pacaud, S.: Experimental research on the aging of psychological functions. In: *Old Age in The Modern World.* E. and S. Livingstone, Edinburgh, Scotland, 1955, pp. 279-289, and Pacaud, S.: Le vierllissement des Aptitudes. In: Benet, L., and Bourliére, F.: *Precis de Gerontologie.* Paris, Masson and Cie, 1955, 40-67.

42. Welford, A. T.: *Aging and Human Skill.* London, Oxford University Press, 1958.

43. Szufron, J.: Experiments on the greater use of vision by older adults. In: *Old Age in the Modern World.* Edinburgh, Scotland, E. and S. Livingstone, 1955, 231-235.

44. Richardson, I. M.: Age and work: A study of 489 men in heavy industry. *Brit. J. Indust. Med., 10:*269-284, 1953.

45. Clark, Le Gros: *The Work Fitness of Older Men.* Report Issued by Nuffield Foundation.

46. King, H. F., and Speakmen, D.: Age and industrial accident rates. *Brit. J. Industrial Med., 10:*51-58, 1953.

47. Whitfield, J. W.: Individual differences in accident susceptibility among coal miners. *Brit. J. Industrial Med., 11:*126-139, 1954.

48. Young, M.L.: Problem Solving Performance in Two Age Groups. In: *Biobehavioral Approach to Intellectual Changes with Aging.* Jarvik, L.F., and Cohen, D., *Psychology and Adult Development and Aging.* Edited by Eisdorfer, C., and Lawton, M.P., copyright American Psychological Association, reprinted by permission. *Journal of Gerontology, 21*:505-510, 1966.

49. Corso, J.F.: Sensory Processes and Age Effects in Normal Adults. In: *Biobehavioral Approach to Intellectual Changes with Aging.* Jarvik, L.F., and Cohen, D., *Psychology of Adult Development and Aging.* Edited by Eisdorfer, C. and Lawton, M.P., copyright 1973 by American Psychological Association, reprinted by permission. *Journal of Gerontology, 26*:90-105, 1971.

50. Botwinick, J., West, R., Storandt, M.: Qualitative Vocabulary test Responses and Age. *Journal of Gerontology, 30:5*, 574-577, September, 1975.

51. Eisdorfer, C., and Wilkie, F.: Intellectual Changes, Normal Aging II. *Reports from Duke Longitudinal Studies,* 1970-73, edited by Palmore E., Duke University Press, 1974, 95-115, by permission.

52. Eisdorfer, C., and Wilkie, F.: Terminal Changes in Intelligence, Normal Aging II. *Reports from Duke Longitudinal Studies,* 1970-73, edited by Palmore, E., Duke University Press, 1974, 103-115, by permission.

53. Birkhill, Wm. R., and Schaie, K.W.: The Effect of Differential Reinforcement of Cautiousness on Intellectual Performance Among the Elderly. *Journal of Gerontology, 30:5*, 578-583, September, 1975.

54. Harkins, S.W., Nowlin, J.B., Ramm, D., and Schroeder S.: Effects of Age, Sex and Time of Watch on a Brief Continuous Performance Task, Normal Aging II. *Reports from Duke Longitudinal Studies,* 1970-73, edited by Palmore, E., Duke University Press, 1974, 140-150, by permission.

55. Bekker, L.D., and Taylor, C.: Attitudes Toward the Aged in a Multi-Generational Sample. *Journal of Gerontology, 21*:115-118, 1966.

56. Cameron, P.: Age Parameter of Young Adults, Middle Aged, Old and Aged. *Journal of Gerontology, 24*:201-202, 1969.

57. Jyrkila, F.: Society and Adjustment to Old Age. In: *Transactions of the Westermarck Society,* volume 5, Turku, Munkgaard, 1960.

## General References

1. Anderson, J. E.: Dynamics of development. In: Harris, D. B. (ed.) : *The Concept of Development*. Minneapolis, U. of Minnesota Press, 1957, 25-46.

2. Babinsky, B.: An analysis of the mental factors of various age groups from nine to sixty. *Genet. Psychol. Monogr., 23:191-234*, 1941.

3. Bayley, Nancy, and Oden, Melita: The maintenance of intellectual ability in gifted adults. *J. Gerontology, 10:91-107*, 1955.

4. Belbin, R. M.: Difficulties of older people in industry. *Occupational Psychol., 27:117-190*, 1953.

5. Bromley, D. B.: Some experimental tests on the effect of age on creative intellectual output. *J. Gerontology, 11:74-82*, 1956.

6. Clark, S. D.: *The Employability of Older Workers*. Ottawa, Canada, Economics and Research Branch, Department of Labor, 1959.

7. Cohen, J.: The factor structure of the WAIS between early adulthood and old age. *J. Consult. Psychol., 21:283-290*, 1957.

8. Cumming, Elaine, and Henry, W. I.: *Growing Old*. New York, Basic Books Inc., 1961.

9. Deutsch, H.: Psychoanalyse der weiblichen sexual Functionen, Neue Arbeiten Zur Ärzlichen Psychoanalyse, vol. 5. Leipzig, Internationaler Psychoanalytischer Verlag, 1925.

10. Goldstein, K., and Scheerer, M.: Abstract and concrete behavior: An experimental study with special tests. *Psychol. Monogr., 53:1-151*, 1941.

11. Jones, H. E.: Intelligence and problem solving. In: Birren, J. E. (ed.) : *Handbook of Aging and The Individual*. Chicago, U. of Chicago Press, 1959, pp. 700-738.

12. Kaplan, O. J.: *Mental Disorders of Later Life*. Stanford, Calif., Stanford U. Press, 1956.

13. Korchin, S. J., and Basowitz, H.: Age differences in verbal learning. *J. Abnormal and Social Psychol., 54:64-69*, 1957.

14. Lehman, H. C.: *Age and Achievement*. Princeton, Princeton U. Press, 1953.

15. Lorge, I., and Tuckman, J.: Attitudes towards older people. *J. Psychol., 37:249-260*, 1953.

16. Lorge, I.: Old age and aging: Psychometry: The evaluation of mental status as a function of the mental test. *Am. J. Orthopsychiat., 10: 56-61*, 1940.

17. Marsh, B. W.: Aging and driving. *Traffic Engineering, 3-21*, Nov. 1960.

18. Norman, J. G.: *Road Traffic Accidents,* Geneva, World Health Organization, 1962, No. 12.

19. Owens, W. A., Jr.: Age and mental abilities: A longitudinal study. *Genetic Psychol. Monogr., 48:3-54*, 1953.

20. Ruch, F. L.: The differentiative effect of age upon human learning. *J. Genetic Psychol., 11*:261-286, 1934.
21. Strong, E. K.: *Change of Interests with Age.* Stanford, Cal., Stanford U. Press, 1931.
22. Tolman, E. C.: *Purposive Behavior in Animals and Men.* New York, Appleton-Century Crafts, 1932.
23. U. S. Department of Labor: *Job Performance and Age: A Study of Measurement,* Washington, D. C., Government Printing Office, Bureau of Labor Statistics, 1956, Bull. No. 1203.
24. U. S. Department of Health, Education and Welfare: *Suicide.* Washington, D. C., Government Printing Office, Vol. 43, No. 30, 1956.
25. Wimer, R. E.: Age differences in incidental and intentional learning. *J. Gerontology, 15*:79-82, 1960.

# Chapter IV

## PSYCHOPATHOLOGY OF AGING

### STATISTICS

CHANGES IN LONGEVITY and mortality rates have had a direct effect upon the prevalence of mental disease. The incidence of mental disease as measured by first admissions to a mental hospital increases from a minimum in childhood to a maximum in old age.

The major causes of institutionalization in mental hospitals are shown in Figure 12. It can be seen that the later life diseases of cerebral arteriosclerosis and senile brain disease comprise the most important category of first hospital admissions, followed by schizophrenia. These figures, however, can be misleading. The average hospital stay of schizophrenic patients is four times longer than that of seniles; thus, their incidence in mental hospitals is much greater than that of seniles. The schizophrenic population in mental hospitals is about half that of all mental patients, whereas the senile group is probably between 10% and 15%. Sensory changes in late life may amplify the incidence of mental illness; for example, a high proportion of older paranoid schizophrenics are found to have auditory or visual defects which contribute to their emotional illness.

During the period from 1946-54, the number of patients in the state and county mental hospitals increased at an average annual rate of 2.1%. Despite changing attitudes toward mental illness resulting in the return of more patients to the community, the rates of net release were still not sufficiently high to counterbalance an increasing number of admissions. A major drop in the patient population occurred in 1955-56 when psychotropic drugs became widespread in the patient population. This decrease in inpatient population has continued up to the present so that currently the resident population is about 50% of its peak in 1955.

## Environment

According to the latest figures on urban vs. rural setting, approximately 85% of first admissions of patients over 60 to mental hospitals are from an urban environment and 15% from a rural environment, the majority of the latter from a non-farm environment. Since about 75% of people over 60 are from an urban setting, the urban population is over-represented among first admissions while the rural population is under represented. The farm population consists of about 5% of the total population while only 2% of first admissions of people over 60 came from the farms. Thus, the incidence of farm population is very small even relative to the total population of people over 60 who live on farms.

**PERCENTAGE OF FIRST ADMISSIONS TO PUBLIC MENTAL**

**HOSPITALS BY CAUSE -- 1963**

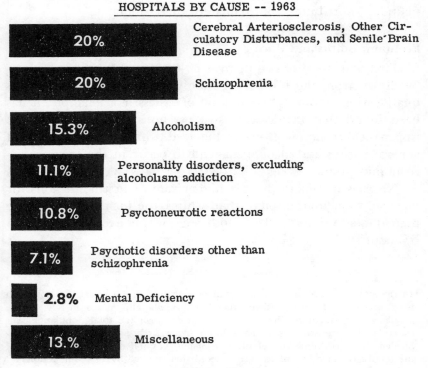

| | |
|---|---|
| 20% | Cerebral Arteriosclerosis, Other Circulatory Disturbances, and Senile Brain Disease |
| 20% | Schizophrenia |
| 15.3% | Alcoholism |
| 11.1% | Personality disorders, excluding alcoholism addiction |
| 10.8% | Psychoneurotic reactions |
| 7.1% | Psychotic disorders other than schizophrenia |
| 2.8% | Mental Deficiency |
| 13.% | Miscellaneous |

Figure 12.

## Marital Status

The majority of aged first admissions to mental hospitals are either married or widowed. In relation to their incidence in the total population, the unmarried aged exceed their quota,* the married do not reach their quota, and the widowed exceed their quota in regard to first admissions to mental hospitals. The separated do not quite reach their quota while the divorced nearly double their quota.

## Education

About 60% of first admissions 60' years and over have attended elementary school, 20% have no formal education, 15% have a high school education, and about 5% have a college education. Again, according to the latest Federal Census figures, the illiterate group exceeds its quota by about 90% while the remainder contributes approximately their quota.

## Economic Status and Race

First admission of people over 60 to mental hospitals seem to be drawn from the lower economic groups although this needs qualification according to the kind of illness. For example, it has been found that manic-depressive psychosis is drawn from the upper socio-economic group in the aged, while on the other hand general paresis and alcoholism tend to occur in the lower socio-economic group.

Negroes in general have a higher rate of first admissions for the aged to mental hospitals than whites, the incidence exceeding their quota by about 110%, and foreign whites exceed their quota by about 10%.

---

*In the statistical discussion of aged and mental disease, the terms "do not reach their quota," and "exceed their quota" are used. This refers merely to the incidence of this group compared to the incidence in the total population. For example, if there are 10% of aged blind living in a particular state and the incidence of aged blind first admitted to mental hospitals in that state is 20% of the total aged, then the blind aged "exceed their quota" by 10% (or double).

## SOCIOLOGICAL ASPECTS

Social factors in the psychopathology of the aged are intimately entwined with constitutional makeup, economic and familial conditions, the emotional content of the people involved, self concept, and the various kinds of reactions to life experience.

### Institutional Changes

In recent years, there have been changes in the structure of the family. The larger family unit consisting of grandparents, parents, and children is not now extant. The reduced size of the family is the product of the economic changes which have taken place in our society, and the development of large cities, reduced numbers of people living in the same house, and ease of transportation has led to greater mobility among people. Until very recently, our economic structure tended to stress the desirability of employing younger people. This now is in the process of a rapid change. Up till very recently, older people who are parents and who have supported themselves in previous years find many of their props — their homes, children, possessions, and friends — suddenly taken from them and their psychic and emotional security is first undermined. Thus, these people experience a cycle of emotional insecurity of childhood to an emotional insecurity of old age. However, in the emotional insecurity of childhood there is a future, with a possibility of overcoming it, while in the emotional insecurity of old age there is only a past, and again, up till very recently, it was only this past which the elderly had to make a liveable present. Now, various governmental and private institutions have given additional benefits such as Medicare and enhanced Social Security benefits.

The high rate of divorce with the concomitant disintegration of the family has led to severe problems among the elderly. Approximately 50% of divorced people eventually remarry. However, it is undoubtedly the remaining 50% which contribute so much to the psychopathology of the aging.

Many of the difficulties of the aged stems from the cultural attitude of society toward older people. Dunham (1) characterizes this attitude as "urban" and a city product, arising from an industrial milieu where age brings lowered productive capacity, decreasing income, a contraction of talents and abilities, and an increased reliance upon one's children. This attitude (which again is in a state of flux) is divorced sharply from the attitude of reverence for the aged in, let us say, Asian countries such as China. In the Chinese society, older people have their status assured and thus there is not the fertile ground for the breeding of insecurity. Aged people need love, affection, and the feeling of being useful and wanted, but up until very recently, the functioning of cultural forces has set them apart, separating them from their families where their needs would be met.

Belknap and Friedsam (2) have attempted to isolate the social factors which play a role in the production of mental disorders of the aged. They believe that social forces have a great influence in the incidence of mental disorders in later life. They consider sex and age as two of the variables which can be correlated with the incidence of mental disease. Belknap suggests for both men and women that when spatial and social mobility are at a minimum, when there is no change in status of the person involved, or with males at a maximum length and with females accompanied by a newly sanctioned status, and if family intergenerational continuity is maintained, mental disorders in later life should be at a minimum. The essence of Belknap's hypothesis is that abrupt status changes in the lives of older people brought about by changes in familial or other social institutions, result in mental disorder.

## Psychological Aspects

The primary psychological aspects of aging have been discussed in the previous chapter. Other variables more directly related to psychopathology will be given here.

### Awareness of Aging

Giese (3) asked subjects when they first noticed they were growing old. Twice as many physical symptoms were mentioned as mental ones. However, educated people are more likely to have mental symptoms. Men more frequently mention they are less potent sexually and both men and women suddenly realize they are no longer young.

Jones (4) found that the average age of becoming subjectively old is 49 years, with a range of 18-82, again with educated people showing a higher percentage of mental symptoms than uneducated ones. Physiological deficit seems to be a minor element in the occurrence of mental disorders of the aged. More important are the cumulative effects of experience, frustrations and awareness of limitations rather than consequences of physiological problems.

## Happiness

Landis (5) attempted to discover the happiest period of life of 450 individuals over 65. Seven per cent were unable to make a choice, 50% named the period between 25-45 as the happiest, 20% chose the years between 18-25 and 18% thought childhood to contain the happiest moments, while only 5% selected middle and old age. The chief sources of reported happiness were marriage and family living, although the majority who chose young adulthood as the happiest period were influenced by finances and health. Kuhlen (6) asked adults ranging from 20-80 to draw a line on a chart indicating happiness levels at various periods of life. Happiness ratings were highest in the first two adult decades, declining soon thereafter.

Graney (Marshall A.) reports on a four year longitudinal study of sixty women ages 60-89 years of age. Data about their happiness and social activities were collected, using the Affect Balance Scale, and nine measures of socially relevant activities, including three measures of media use, three interpersonal interaction and three activities in voluntary associations. There was a direct relationship between happiness and social activity. Increase in activity over time was often related to happiness and declines in activity were related to unhappiness. Face to face interaction was highly related to unhappiness. Of all the mass media only radio listening was related to happiness.

Happiness, of course, is intimately intertwined with the self concept. At the Duke Center for the Study of Aging and Human Development, a study by Back (Kurt W.) found that personally

Graney, Marshall A. — Happiness and Social Participation in aging. *Journal of Gerontology—30*:106, 701-706, 1975.

achieved positions and characteristics as well as personal values become important with age. It may be that freed from family obligations, women can much more easily be accepted for what they are. Men on the other hand are involved in the work role much more personally, and difficulties with this role through aging may make things even more difficult for them.

## Sexuality

The recurrence of overt and strong physical sexuality in the aged is a phenomenon not explained on a purely physiological basis. It appears to be a compensating element representing the older person's rebellion against the onset of old age, of which fading sexuality is a stereotype. Hamilton (7) reports an increase in masturbation in the 7th decade as compared with the 50's and 60's. Analysts offer an explanation for senile sexuality in terms of the increased libidinal drives arising from an unconscious desire to have offspring.

Pfeiffer (Eric) Verwoerdt (Adriaan) and Davis (Glenn C.), studied 261 male subjects aged 45-69. 98% were married, 1% widowed and 1% never married, and 241 women in this age range were also studied. 71% were married, 18% widowed, 5% never married and 6% separated or divorced. The following areas of sexual behavior were assessed.

1. Enjoyment of sexual relations in younger years.
2. Enjoyment of sexual relations at the present time.
3. Sexual feeling in younger years.
4. Sexual feelings at the present time.
5. Frequency of sexual relations in younger years.
6. Frequency of sexual relations at the present time.
7. Awareness of any decline in sexual interest or activity. If there was any, at what age was it first noted.
8. If sexual relations have stopped, when were they stopped!
9. Reason for stopping sexual relations.

There were dramatic differences between men and women of like age in regard to practically all indications of sexual behavior with the men reporting greater interest and activity than women. Where there was an overall pattern of decline of interest and activity with advancing age, it was clear that sex still continued to play an important role in the lives of the vast majority of the subjects studied. 6% of the men and 33% of the women said they were no longer interested in sex. 12% of the men and 44% of the women said they no longer had sexual relations. By age 50, 49% of the men and 58% of the women admitted they had noted some decline in their sexual interest and activity. By age 70, 88% of the men and 96% of the women admitted an awareness of such a decline occurred between the 45-50 group and the 50-55 group.

Some 14% of the men and 40% of the women indicated they had stopped having sexual relations and offered reasons for having done so. It was rather interesting that women overwhelmingly attribute responsibility for cessation of sexual relations to their husbands, while men hold themselves responsible for cessation.

Statistically, homosexual acts of older men with small boys are common, but there is an absence of offenses against mature women, which is explained as the sublimation of the sexual drive or as part of an effort to regain lost youth by identification. Adult sex gratification is not as common as immature sex play and genital manipulation. One of the difficulties in ascertaining statistics concerning senile sex offenders is that they do not find their way into the courts. Senile men constitute about 5% of all male sex offenders, but when sexual offenses against children are considered they constitute about 12% of the total offenses.

## Crimes

Figures 13-16 and Tables 9 and 10 show the percentage of various crimes in 1962 in various age groups as reported by the F.B.I. Arrests by age group and top 20 crimes, and age grouping and arrests in 1964. Crime rates for offenses of all kinds decrease after middle life. Rape tends to be a young man's crime; about 35% of the arrests for rape are in the under 20 group and about 58% in the 20-29 and only 8% in the group over age 40. Likewise, impulsive crimes such as automobile thefts occur primarily among youth under 20 while counterfeiting and forgery, which require premeditation and experience occur in the older group. Employment is also a factor in crime insofar as age is concerned. In men 25-35, there is a tendency for arrests for property offenses to be

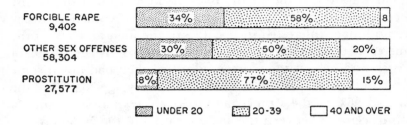

Figure 13. Age and the percentages of arrests for sex offenses, 1962. *Source:* U.S. Department of Justice: *Crime in the United States.* Uniform Crime Reports, 1962. Washington, D.C., Federal Bureau of Investigation, 1963.

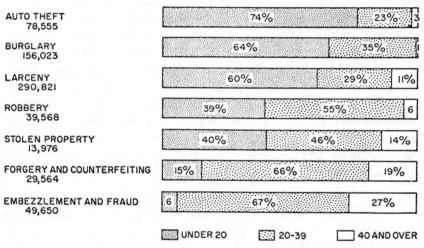

Figure 14. Age and the percentage of arrests for types of stealing, 1962. *Source: Ibid.*

related to unemployment, while the reverse is true for youths under 17; the assumption is that during unemployment the 25-35 group have great economic pressures and insecurity. However, in the 35 and older group, the crime rate decreases during unemployment. The explanation for this is that during unemployment older men spend more time with their families and there are more tightly organized family patterns.

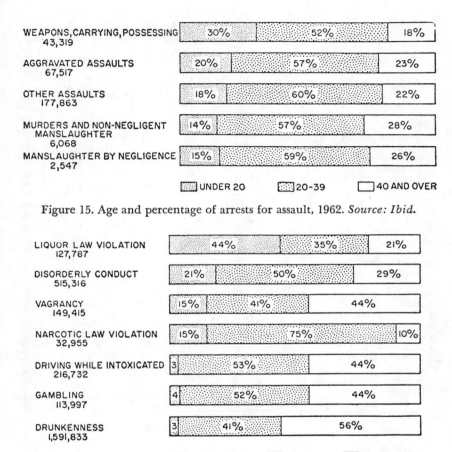

Figure 15. Age and percentage of arrests for assault, 1962. *Source: Ibid.*

Figure 16. Age and the percentage of arrests for vice and conduct violations, 1962. *Source: Ibid.*

The whole problem of crime in the elderly is complicated by the fact that there is a tendency for many judges and juries to be lenient with older criminals especially if the criminal is of an advanced age.

The explanation of crime in the older person is not yet complete. It has been suggested that senile personality changes are the cause of such offenses as calumny, embezzlement, fraud, forgery,

TABLE 9

ARRESTS BY AGE GROUP (5-YEAR PERIODS)
UNIFORM CRIME REPORTS, 1964

| Offense | 25-29 | 50-54 | 55-59 | 60-64 | 65 and above |
|---|---|---|---|---|---|
| Criminal homicide | | | | | |
| a) Murder | 1,009 | 361 | 149 | 126 | 106 |
| b) Manslaughter | 380 | 169 | 63 | 42 | 64 |
| Forcible rape | 1,529 | 126 | 51 | 25 | 27 |
| Robbery | 5,365 | 302 | 89 | 61 | 48 |
| Aggravated assault | 11,479 | 3,322 | 1,536 | 938 | 885 |
| Burglary | 14,453 | 1,383 | 536 | 253 | 162 |
| Larceny | 22,006 | 7,234 | 3,621 | 2,406 | 2,182 |
| Auto theft | 4,228 | 368 | 122 | 53 | 30 |
| *Subtotal* | 60,449 | 13,265 | 6,167 | 3,904 | 3,504 |
| Other assaults | 28,842 | 7,373 | 3,096 | 1,729 | 1,566 |
| Arson | 256 | 89 | 49 | 26 | 33 |
| Forgery, counterfeiting | 5,110 | 837 | 314 | 130 | 95 |
| Fraud | 8,474 | 2,073 | 805 | 453 | 294 |
| Embezzlement | 1,621 | 380 | 149 | 54 | 62 |
| Stolen property | 1,934 | 360 | 178 | 86 | 70 |
| Vandalism | 2,283 | 454 | 241 | 146 | 161 |
| Weapons, carrying | 6,173 | 1,642 | 731 | 458 | 421 |
| Prostitution | 5,884 | 638 | 228 | 163 | 135 |
| Sex Offenses | 6,999 | 2,088 | 1,095 | 740 | 843 |
| Narcotic drug laws | 6,645 | 504 | 203 | 111 | 67 |
| Gambling | 13,614 | 10,108 | 5,446 | 3,795 | 3,584 |
| Offenses against family | 10,901 | 2,070 | 703 | 276 | 238 |
| Driving under the influence | 26,928 | 22,199 | 11,222 | 6,086 | 3,864 |
| Liquor laws | 7,097 | 5,591 | 2,903 | 1,852 | 1,377 |
| Drunkenness | 116,731 | 189,609 | 103,528 | 69,053 | 52,221 |
| Disorderly conduct | 52,596 | 25,588 | 12,729 | 8,804 | 7,318 |
| Vagrancy | 11,340 | 13,388 | 7,786 | 5,482 | 4,325 |
| All other offenses | 51,551 | 18,772 | 8,540 | 5,731 | 5,427 |
| Suspicion | 11,951 | 3,289 | 1,719 | 1,040 | 825 |
| *Total* | 437,379 | 320,317 | 167,832 | 110,119 | 86,430 |

and narcotics crimes.

Hentig (8) states:

"The criminality of the older man resembles in many ways that of the woman. He is the instigator or he commits crimes in which craftiness or the use of physical or chemical forces play a role. At the same time, feeling that the normal methods of defeating a competitor are not any longer at his disposal, the older man falls back on primitive means of violence. Even the weak can use force if he chooses a weaker object, a woman or child, or if he teams to strength-saving devices, weapons, poison, and deceit. Arson is one of the crimes with a high old age rate."

TABLE 10
"TOP 20" CRIMES BY AGE GROUPING AND ARRESTS—1964

| Age Group 25-29 | Arrests | Age Group 50-54 | Arrests |
|---|---|---|---|
| 1. Drunkeness | 116,731 | 1. Drunkeness | 186,609 |
| 2. Disorderly Conduct | 52,596 | 2. Disorderly Conduct | 25,588 |
| 3. All other offenses | 51,551 | 3. Driving under inf. | 22,199 |
| 4. Other assaults | 28,842 | 4. All other offenses | 18,772 |
| 5. Driving under inf. | 26,928 | 5. Vagrancy | 13,388 |
| 6. Larceny (theft) | 22,006 | 6. Gambling | 10,108 |
| 7. Burglary | 14,453 | 7. Other assaults | 7,373 |
| 8. Gambling | 13,614 | 8. Larceny | 7,234 |
| 9. Suspicion | 11,951 | 9. Liquor Laws | 5,591 |
| 10. Aggravated assault | 11,479 | 10. Aggravated assault | 3,322 |
| 11. Vagrancy | 11,340 | 11. Suspicion | 3,289 |
| 12. Offenses against family | 10,901 | 12. Sex Offenses | 2,088 |
| 13. Fraud | 8,474 | 13. Fraud | 2,073 |
| 14. Narcotics | 7,645 | 14. Offenses against family | 2,070 |
| 15. Liquor Laws | 7,097 | 15. Weapons | 1,642 |
| 16. Sex offenses | 6,999 | 16. Burglary | 1,383 |
| 17. Weapons | 6,173 | 17. Forgery and counterfeiting | 837 |
| 18. Prostitution, com. vice | 5,884 | 18. Prostitution, com. vice | 638 |
| 19. Robbery | 5,365 | 19. Narcotics | 504 |
| 20. Forgery and counterfeiting | 5,110 | 20. Vandalism | 454 |

| Age Group 55-59 | Arrests | Age Group 60-64 | Arrests |
|---|---|---|---|
| 1. Drunkeness | 103,528 | 1. Drunkenness | 69,053 |
| 2. Disorderly Conduct | 12,729 | 2. Disorderly conduct | 8,804 |
| 3. Driving under infl. | 11,222 | 3. Driving under infl. | 6,086 |
| 4. All other offenses | 8,540 | 4. All other offenses | 5,731 |
| 5. Vagrancy | 7,786 | 5. Vagrancy | 5,482 |
| 6. Gambling | 5,446 | 6. Gambling | 3,795 |
| 7. Larceny | 3,621 | 7. Larceny | 2,406 |
| 8. Other assaults | 3,096 | 8. Liquor laws | 1,852 |
| 9. Liquor laws | 2,903 | 9. Other assaults | 1,729 |
| 10. Suspicion | 1,719 | 10. Suspicion | 1,040 |
| 11. Aggravated assault | 1,536 | 11. Aggravated assault | 938 |
| 12. Sex offenses | 1,095 | 12. Sex offenses | 740 |
| 13. Fraud | 805 | 13. Weapons | 458 |
| 14. Weapons | 731 | 14. Fraud | 453 |
| 15. Offenses against family | 703 | 15. Offenses against family | 276 |
| 16. Burglary | 536 | 16. Burglary | 253 |
| 17. Forgery and counterfeiting | 314 | 17. Prostitution and com. vice | 163 |
| 18. Vandalism | 241 | 18. Vandalism | 146 |
| 19. Prostitution and com. vice | 228 | 19. Forgery and counterfeiting | 130 |
| 20. Stolen property, receiving | 178 | 20. Criminal homicide | 126 |

| Age Group 65 and over | Arrests | Age Group 65 and over | Arrests |
|---|---|---|---|
| 1. Drunkenness | 52,221 | 11. Sex offenses | 843 |
| 2. Disorderly conduct | 7,318 | 12. Suspicion | 825 |
| 3. All other offenses | 5,527 | 13. Weapons, carrying | 421 |
| 4. Vagrancy | 4,325 | 14. Fraud | 294 |
| 5. Driving under influence | 3,864 | 15. Offenses against family | 238 |
| 6. Gambling | 3,584 | 16. Burglary | 162 |
| 7. Larceny | 2,182 | 17. Vandalism | 161 |
| 8. Other assaults | 1,566 | 18. Prostitution and com. vice | 135 |
| 9. Liquor laws | 1,377 | 19. Criminal homicide | 106 |
| 10. Aggravated assault | 885 | 20. Forgery and counterfeiting | 95 |

### Suicide

Figure 17 indicates the suicide rate by age, sex, and race. As can be seen, men are more vulnerable to suicide than women in later life, and the gap widens with advancing chronological age particularly in the white race. Precipitants such as physical infirmity, chronic illness or the diagnosis of an incurable disease seem to be more potent in older men than women. The suicides of older men are usually of a violent nature and leave little doubt that they were intentional. Women on the other hand seem to be more passive in their attempts and record more unsuccessful attempts than do men.

An interesting side light of the suicide rate is that of race. The suicide rate of non-whites of both sexes is lower than in whites, and the rate differences are more pronounced in later life than in early adulthood. Southern Negroes have a lower suicide rate than Negroes residing elsewhere in the United States. It is possible that insofar as the Negro is concerned, he became inured to poverty and hardship and finds these disabilities less weighty as time goes on than the white, and the Southern Negro less so than the Northern. A tentative explanation for the difference in suicide rate between whites and non-whites is that the culture surrounding non-whites encourages an outward aggressive pattern rather than an inward one.

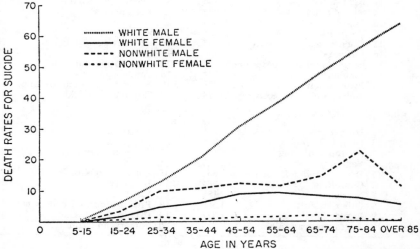

Figure 17. Suicide death rates by age, sex and race. *Source:* USDHEW. *Special Reports.* Washington, D.C., Bureau of Vital Statistics, 1956.

SUICIDE MORTALITY RATES, BY SEX, RACE, AND AGE GROUPS: 1950 to 1970
(Rate per 100,000 Population)

| AGE | MALE | | | | | | FEMALE | | | | | |
|---|---|---|---|---|---|---|---|---|---|---|---|---|
| | White | | | Negro & Other | | | White | | | Negro & Other | | |
| | 1950 | 1960 | 1970 | 1950 | 1960 | 1970 | 1950 | 1960 | 1970 | 1950 | 1960 | 1970 |
| Total... | 19.0 | 17.6 | 18.0 | 7.0 | 7.2 | 8.5 | 5.5 | 5.3 | 7.1 | 1.7 | 2.0 | 2.0 |
| 5-14 ....... | 0.3 | 0.5 | 0.5 | 0.1 | 0.1 | 0.2 | 0.1 | 0.1 | 0.1 | 0.1 | — | 0.1 |
| 15-24 ....... | 6.6 | 8.6 | 13.9 | 5.3 | 5.3 | 11.3 | 2.7 | 2.3 | 4.2 | 1.7 | 1.5 | 4.1 |
| 25-34 ....... | 13.8 | 14.9 | 19.9 | 10.1 | 12.9 | 19.8 | 5.2 | 5.8 | 9.0 | 2.8 | 3.5 | 5.8 |
| 35-44 ....... | 22.4 | 21.9 | 23.3 | 11.3 | 13.5 | 12.6 | 8.2 | 8.1 | 13.0 | 2.2 | 3.7 | 4.3 |
| 45-54 ....... | 34.1 | 33.7 | 29.5 | 11.7 | 12.8 | 14.1 | 10.5 | 10.9 | 13.5 | 4.0 | 3.2 | 4.5 |
| 55-64 ....... | 45.9 | 40.2 | 35.0 | 16.8 | 16.9 | 10.5 | 10.7 | 10.9 | 12.3 | 1.2 | 3.4 | 2.2 |
| 65 and over . | 55.8 | 46.7 | 41.1 | 13.3 | 12.4 | 10.8 | 9.9 | 8.8 | 8.5 | 2.4 | 3.9 | 3.6 |

- Represents zero

Source: U.S. National Center for Health Statistics, published in *Statistical Abstract of the United States*, U.S. Department of Commerce, Social and Economic Statistics Administration, Bureau of the Census.

TABLE 10A

## DESCRIPTION OF PSYCHOPATHOLOGICAL CONDITIONS

There is an inherent difficulty in using the psychiatric patterns of the Diagnostic and Statistical Manual of Mental Disorders prepared by the American Psychiatric Association in 1967, since this classification system is continually changing. However, in general, this text will adhere to this system in a description of those diagnostic categories important to aging, although all these categories will not be discussed, but only those that have an etiological relationship to the aging process and those which have serious impact upon the individual.

### NEUROSES

There is nothing greatly different in the neurotic patterns one finds in later maturity as distinguished from those in early life. The modifications which are seen can be attributed to both biological aging and the peculiar status given to older people in our society. The neuroses of aging persons, just like those of younger people, represent unsuccessful attempts to adapt to personal difficulties, and it is most probable that the aged who develop neurotic reactions in the latter part of life have had similar maladaptations under stress when they were younger. There are certain antecedent and concurrent factors which are responsible for the development of neurotic maladjustment in later life.

**Physical Dysfunctions**

*1. Vision and Hearing.** Fading vision and hearing tends to isolate older people from participation in activities of his social group. The total or partially deaf and blind are given to paranoid suspicion and the real motives of a real social community become suspicious, distorted and imagined motives of a pseudocommunity. This kind of sensory impairment will often exacerbate long standing neurotic impairments.

*2. Visceral Dysfunctions.* Old visceral organs are seldom able to function the way they did in their younger years, and the resultant dysfunctions make older people anxious, discontented, narcissistic with a tendency to complain about themselves. If the person has had a reaction pattern earlier in life in reacting with hypochondriacal behavior as a response to frustration and disappointment, it is likely to appear in later life in exaggerated form. This may account for the hypochondriacal fear of malignant neoplasms which many people develop in later life.

*3. Sexual Factors.* As stated on p. 98, crimes of a sexual nature do occur in older people. Hamilton (9) found a marked reduction in potency among his patients in the 50's and 60's. However, the reactions to a declining sexual potency are many and varied. Sexual adventures which are an aggressive compensation at gaining assurance of the person's sexual competence are quite frequent. When these adventures fail, the older person may anticipate failure, ostracism, or even social retaliation and may cause him fear, guilt, and great anxiety, which may lead to neurotic reactive depressions.

A form in the whole area of neuroses which *social* restriction of the sexual behavior of older people may take, is resentment of manifestation of sexual activity in others. It exhibits itself in being morally indignant at the excesses and depravity of modern youth and people in general. Here, a constant preoccupation with sex can emerge in what appears to be a socially acceptable form.

Fantasy is a mode of adjustment to frustration and privation and the aged resort to sexual fantasies for gratification just as they did in adolescence and childhood. There arises a vicious circle of forbidden fantasies, autoeroticism and then anxiety, feelings of

*See pp. 66-73,;74, 75, supra.

worthlessness, hypochondriacal concern with the genitals and ultimately depression. Baker and Wilensky (10) found that older people do fantasize about erotic drives but are unwilling to admit this.

*4. Reduction in Strength and Endurance.* The realization of the inevitable loss of strength and endurance in senescence may come as the result of illness, injury, or in competition with younger people. The results of this realization may take two forms. The aged person will give up completely and too easily with symptoms of weakness, nervousness, fatigability, incapacity, and visceral disorders. On the other hand, he may refuse to accept his waning biological status and try to show he is just as good as any one else and insist on his competence and make frequent comparisons between himself and the younger generation. Sometimes, there is an extremely aggressive compensatory activity exhibited by restlessness, sleeplessness, and irritability with frequent resort to alcohol. These people usually "give up," and when this happens, they fall back on all sorts of hypochondriacal complaints, headaches, visceral disorders, lack of appetite, etc. Some older people who hiterto have taken pride in their bodily vigor, embark on rigorous physical culture routines when this vigor begins to diminish. Thus, a strong interest in health in older people may have its causal roots in an attempt to deny an inevitable decline in physique.

*5. Other Biological Factors.* The decrease in sensory and perceptual acuity,* neural and humoral coordination, secretary responses, tonic and phasic action, muscle and bone atrophy, and reduction in subcutaneous and bulbar fat and decrease in elasticity of the skin all have great emotional significance to the aging person. These coupled with reduction in drives and gratifications and common visceral dysfunctions threaten the security of the senescent. In women, where the retention of a youthful appearance is so important to her status, the fading of these physical attributes may be a serious personal threat. When an aging woman's attempt to cover up her age by cosmetics fails, she may resort to malaise, fatigue, and various kinds of visceral complaints as a defense mechanism. When these complaints do indeed succeed in bring-

---

*See pp. 65-73

ing back the attention and consideration which her attractiveness formerly earned, they are likely to be organized into an unconscious neurotic pattern. Just how much of a threat the fading biological processes and what form they will take in all aging people will depend very much on how well these aged have weathered other biological threats and other stress situations in earlier life.

There is one disease which bears special mention in discussing the biological aspects of aging.

1) Heart Disease — Heart disease is one of the most common causes of death in old age. According to the 1969 statistics published by the U.S. Public Health Service, the mortality rate from heart disease in the age group 65-74 is about 1,700 per 100,000; for the age group 75-84, this rate is more than doubled; among people 85 and above, it is almost six times this high. Almost all these deaths are attributed to rheumatic heart disease or congestive heart failure.* Heart disease is also one of the most serious clinical problems of old age. It is commonly held that brain impairment and heart disease are closely linked in the elderly. Eisdorfer (1967) and Ewalt and Ruskin (1944) have carried on studies consistently linking patients with congenital and rheumatic heart disease and patients undergoing cardiac surgery with a high incidence of cognitive impairment and neuropsychiatric or electroencephalographic abnormalities. Vost, Wolochow, and Howell (1964) in postmortem studies showed histological evidence of cerebral infarction in more than half the patients with old myocardial infarction or hypertensive heart disease; but in only twelve percent of those having no heart disease. In a group of 227 elderly citizens who participated in a longitudinal study at the Duke University Center for the Study of Aging and Human Development, volunteers were given a physical, neurological, and psychiatric examination, together with psychological and psychiatric tests. The volunteers were divided into four groups:

1 — No heart disease (105 subjects)
2 — Questionable heart disease (27 subjects)
3 — Definite and compensated heart disease (47 subjects).

---

*See Geist, H., *The Emotional Aspects of Heart Disease,* Long Island: Libra Publishers, 1976.

4 — Definite and decompensated heart disease (48 subjects)

Brain status was evaluated on the bases of the neurological and EEG examinations and the verbal and performance scaled WAIS scores.

From the evidence from the EEG and neurological findings, the incidence of CNS disorder was much greater in decompensated heart disease, but slightly less in those with compensated heart disease than in those without heart disease. This suggests that brain impairments in old age are related to heart failure due to a reduction of cerebral blood flow. The lack of brain impairment in subjects with compensated heart disease is attributable to the relatively high blood pressure in this group. The findings of this study suggest that in some elderly patients mild hypertension may help to maintain the blood flow to the brain at the expense of the heart. Thus, in some elderly people a raise in the elevation of the blood pressure is a compensatory response to a lack of blood in the brain secondary to hardening of the blood vessels of the brain (cerebral arteriosclerosis). The WAIS scores in patients either with compensated or decompensated heart disease were quite poor related to brain impairment and, in part, to decreased use of the remaining intellectual faculties.

### Psychological Factors

*Loss of Significance.* The greatest changes which the senescent dread is the loss of significance and the loss of independence. The inevitable "taking over" by the younger generation carries with it reduced circumstances and a threat of economic and psychological dependence. This prospect may lead to exaggerated reactions of anxiety, tension, fatigue, and dejection. The oft occurring circumstance where the older person must move from his own home to that of a married child may be very upsetting. Psychoanalysts claim that this now gives the adult offspring a chance at revenge for years of submission and that since this circumstance forces the offspring to give up the role of dependent child and assume a new role of protector and provider the child's resentment toward his parent increases when the latter comes under his jurisdiction.

The uprooting of the aged from their home surroundings may develop into all kinds of psychopathology. Reactive neurotic depressions are quite common. Symptoms of fatigue and incompetence, fantasy, excessive reminiscences, and hypochondriasis are familiar patterns in these people. The loss of significance is extremely important. The advent of retirement may mean "not being on the in" with the company or corporation. It is not finances which usually disturb retirees but the loss of prestige, responsibility, and importance. For many seniles, it is no easier to sit on the sidelines unnoticed by others than it is for the adolescent wallflower. The appearance of neurotic behavior under conditions of decreasing influence and authority will depend on how suddenly the change in prestige took place, upon the position he had previously, and the degree of importance or prestige accorded to him in the present. Such lost prestige may give rise to neurotic aggression, hypochondriasis, anxiety, rejection, negation, and revenge.

**Anxiety States**

The anxiety states experienced by people in later life are much the same as those experienced in earlier life and are not exactly new to the neurotic senescent. The anxiety may permeate the thoughts and behavior of the individual and is usually of the "free floating" type. It is characterized by physiological derivatives of strong emotional reactions with such symptoms as overbreathing, increased skeletal tensions, visceral disturbances, tremors, headaches, perspiring, nausea, diarrhea, and a sense of impending danger. The older person will worry about all sorts of things. The attacks of acute anxiety may occur without any apparent precipitating event and the elderly individual may be convinced that they are seriously ill and there is impending death. Conscious precipitants are guilt reactions coming in the wake of hostile and vengeful fantasies involving their adult offspring, their mate or other people in their environment who are frustrating them. Other conflicts, sexual fantasies, and autoerotic practices are also precipitants. In general the circumstances of later life and maturity which provoke anxiety neurosis are lack of security, circumstances where the older person is less welcome, less useful, less valued, and less dependent on anyone than on his earlier years.*

---

*There is some evidence that childhood reminiscence and what is called the "life review process" is greatly influenced by the current environment of the aged

## Neurotic Depression

Neurotic depressions are distinguished from psychotic depressions by being mild, shallow, brief, less withdrawn from reality, and the patient recognizes that he is not wholly responsible for his loss of self esteem. Depressive periods do increase in frequency and depth in the later years. Busse and his co-workers reported findings in a group of supposedly well-adjusted subjects over the age of 60, and found that in a study of these supposedly well-adjusted subjects, a significant portion reported a definite increase in frequency and depth of depressive episodes. Busse also found that persons above the age of 60 who are from lower socio-economic groups suffered depressions much more frequently than individuals from employed groups. Thus, according to this viewpoint, elderly people who remain gainfully employed tend to be better adjusted than those who are not so occupied. Kutner (11) reports in a community survey on aging that almost one person in eight mentioned prolonged and protracted depression. Very often, such depressions will come as the result of the death or serious illness of relatives, friends, or business associates. Loss plays a particularly important role with regard to depression in the older individual. By its very nature, the aging process involves a progressive loss of loved objects. An increased number of physical impairments is another type of loss which may lead to depression in old age. The elderly person then becomes narcissistic and self-depreciatory with symptoms of fatigue, malaise, and lack of sexual appetite. Irritability, mild aversions, tensions, digestive and visceral disorders may appear and there is a general restless unhappiness. The symptoms may cause great annoyance to others in the environment and there occurs a kind of self-perpetuating cycle because these people are those who may have caused him to feel unhappy and neglected in the first place. Neurotic depression in the elderly tends to be of the reactive type or traceable to a

---

person. For example, Etigson and Tobin found that the stress of institutionalization had a powerful influence on reminiscence in the aged. They examined aged subjects before and after institutionalization in a home for the aged and found that more death themes and morbidity occurred in reminiscences after institutionalization than before. (Tobin, Sheldon S., and Etigson, Elizabeth C.: Effect of Stress on Reminiscence in the Aged. Paper presented at the American Psychological Association Meeting in New York City, September, 1966.)

definite cause or precipitant as opposed to the anxiety reactions.

The relation between depression and physical health was experimentally determined by a project in 1960 at the Duke University Center for the Study of Aging and Human Development. 157 community volunteers, average age 72.3 years, were studied by means of a thorough physical examination, blood test, appraisal of current social activity level, and standardized psychological assessment. On the basis of interviews, each study participant was rated for the severity of depressive symptoms on a 0-5 graduated scale. There were fifty-two individuals who had depressive symptoms, and 105 who had no depressive symptoms. As a follow up, the same individuals who participated in the 1960 study were studied in terms of their physical health characteristics from 1960-1970. A prominent association was shown between depressive feeling states and the individual's subjective and objective health states. This relationship was not transient in nature and persisted over the course of a decade. Two possibilities were suggested by the direction of the project. First, depression can be viewed as providing a substitute for physiological impairment leading to ill health; or, second, ill health may evoke depression.

## PSYCHONEUROSES

### Compulsions

The older psychiatric patient who exhibits compulsions is usually one who has showed them in earlier life. The symptoms in later life (as in earlier) are excessive cleanliness and orderliness, perfectionism, various kinds of rituals, primarily to guard against error, excessive doubting, and excessive use of set phrases and gestures, and complaints of being compelled to do or not to do or say or not say certain things. There is also the checking and rechecking of various safeguards such as doors, locks, gas jets, toilets, and water faucets.

The reasons for the appearance of compulsions in the aged are varied. They may appear as the result of mounting anxiety, insecurity, or inadequacy. They may appear as a symbolic attempt to simplify the environment by stereotyping or restricting one's reaction to it. Or, they may appear in the elderly as a result of erotic, aggressive, or vindictive fantasies which arouse guilt and acute anxiety.

## Hysteria

The kinds of hysterical disorders of the elderly are primarily an exaggeration of an organic defect in the older person such as arthritic dyskineses, lameness, defects in vision and hearing which arouses sympathy or guilt in those around him. When these manifestations do in fact restore a measure of security, or in gaining prestige or attention, they may become dangerously fixed and actually believed by the senescent person.

## Neurasthenia (Nervous Exhaustion or Chronic Fatigue)

The beginnings of neurasthenia or chronic fatigue in later life is difficult to detect because it is usual for the elderly to tire more quickly and recover more slowly than when they were mature adults. Since there is in later maturity a sudden or gradual reduction in the opportunities for rewarding kinds of activities, this lack of gratification can cause fatigue. Thus, the detection of neurasthenia must depend upon many factors, primarily previous energy levels, comparison between complaints and biological age and whether environmental stress is present.

## Hypochondriases

Although hypochondriasis is not a disease entity as such, and not listed in the Diagnostic and Statistical Manual of the American Psychiatric Association, the author believes that this syndrome is so prevalent among the aged that it should be discussed here. Busse (12), in a study of an adult population in a clinic, found that hypochondriasis was found to be more prevalent in elderly patients. Walters and Woltman (13) also report a high incidence of hypochondriasis in people in the declining years of their lives. The hypochondriacal complaints are usually directed at ingestion, digestion, and evacuation but there are often complaints in the reproductive, excretory, cardiovascular, and skeletal systems. The symptomatology of hypochondriasis may take the form of

1) A shift away or withdrawal of the patient's interests from other people or objects around him and a centering of his psychic interests upon himself, his body and its functioning.
2) The "symptoms" in various parts of his body may be used as punishment and partial atonement for guilt resulting from hostile, vengeful feelings against the people close to him.
3) There may be a shift of anxiety from a psychic area to less threatening concern with bodily disease and functioning.

When an older person realizes that he is performing relatively poorly, he begins to think that he may be condemned by society. A method of maintaining self respect is to become sick and thus shift the blame for inadequacy to illness. Under practically all circumstances, hypochondriasis is difficult to live with but it is so much harder when the hypochondriac is an older person because the people around an elderly hypochondriac, usually younger relatives or friends, become enmeshed in a network of annoyance, rejection, and subsequent guilt which comes as a result of concern about neglecting the older person.

## THE PSYCHOSES

### Involutional Psychotic Reactions

Involutional psychotic reactions constitute about 4% of first admissions to public mental hospitals. The involutional psychoses occur in women after 40 and are found in the pre-, intra-, and post-climacteric stages and are quite often associated with the menopause. The characteristic symptoms are restlessness, feelings of discomfort, easy fatigability and somatic complaints. Transitory crying spells and "hot flashes and flushes" occur frequently in females.

In dynamic terms, repressed poorly utilized conflicts and guilt feelings and castration mechanisms appear and there is a gradual restricted range of interests and withdrawal from outside objects and people. This pervasive narcissism is motivated by unsuccessful attempts to punish both themselves and persons about them. An anxious, agitated depression appears and suicidal ideas are common. The patient gradually becomes more worried, has greater difficulty sleeping and as the psychotic pattern continues, delusional ideas, most of them paranoid, develop as a defense against the oncoming psychotic depression. Involutional psychotic reactions are quite common in those older individuals who have shown obsessive compulsive traits all their lives. These people also develop an air of martyrdom and the world is not worthy of them and does not appreciate their sacrifices. A whining, nagging attitude toward the marital partner or physician is also common. Fear, hypochondriacal delusions, and mild hallucinations make up the final gamut of symptoms. Psychotic reactions of the involutional period are more common in females in a ratio of about 8-3 and etiologically is strongly linked to conflicts in the sexual sphere since the menopause is concrete evidence to a woman that her sexual capacities are being diminished. For those women who have not achieved sexual satisfaction, the menopausal period may be symbolic that she is being punished for previous behavior.

## Psychotic Depression

The group of elderly patients who show severe depression not related to involutional changes are usually those where the depression is precipitated by an environmental event, usually some relatively recent life event since these people are particularly vulnerable to this reaction because during the period of old age they are more likely to have more serious and frequent losses to their self esteem and threats to their previous way of life adjustment. The psychotic depressions in the elderly are usually termed "reactive depressions" because they are a reaction to environmental events. The difference between a neurotic depression* and a psychotic one depends upon the extent to which the individual withdraws from reality and the willingness of the patient to recognize that he is not wholly responsible for the loss of his self esteem and that he can be at least partially "cured."

## Manic-Depressive Psychoses

Manic-depressive psychoses in the elderly are characterized by severe mood swings. The manic period is characterized by elation and a great amount of talk, flight of ideas and excessive motor activity followed by a gradual return to normality and then a

---

*See pp. 109, 110 supra

swing to the depressive side, characterized by the opposite kind of behavior. Patients who experience their first attack after 40 have a poorer prognosis for treatment than those who have had an earlier onset. There also seems to be a hereditary factor in the disease, but it is not predictable according to Mendelian laws.

### The Presenile and Senile Dementias

The presenile and senile dementias are those diseases in which organic deterioration of the brain is caused exclusively by senescence. The presenile dementias can be classified into two groups:

a) *Primary*. These are diseases occurring during the years 45-60. Very little is known about their cause.

b) *Secondary*. These are diseases seen at various age periods, but also occur during the years 45-60. The dementia is caused by a known etiological agent. In this secondary group, the clinicopathological picture is that of the original condition which is the essential cause of the disease; the age factor is unimportant.

The presenile and senile dementias are more common in women than men, the ratio being 2:1.

Busse and Wang, in their studies at the Duke University Center for the Study of Aging and Human Development, found that in addition to the factors that affect the brain directly, many other factors contribute to dementia (e.g., pulmonary disease, blood pressure, type and amount of activities (or inactivity), pre-existing personality patterns, emotional disorders, socio-economic status, and institutionalization.

### Alzheimer's Disease

This illness was described by Alois Alzheimer in 1906, and in 1907 he published the first clinical and pathological description of the disease. The incidence among women is greater than that among men (3:2) and the average age of onset is about 55 years. Its cause is unknown. However in this current age where a great deal of attention is being paid to the neurological consequences of slow viruses—viruses which have a lag of weeks to years between infection and clinical expression and this kind of agent insofar as etiology is concerned cannot be ruled out. It is.characterized by rapidly progressive mental deterioration with loss of memory and illogical reasoning although insight in these patients is usually preserved. The clinical picture can be divided into three stages:

*Stage 1.* The intellectual deterioration becomes apparent by impairment in ability to calculate and there is impairment in logical reasoning. There are also a defective perception and comprehension of abstract material and a marked loss of memory for recent events. A gradual depressive reaction takes place with anxiety and irritability. Mild paranoid trends gradually appear and there is a distressing awareness of impending insanity. In this initial stage, alterations of speech mechanisms are frequent with such events as the forgetting of words, difficult pronunciation, errors in writing and reading and occasionally epileptic attacks will occur. Occasionally, there are anti-social and immoral acts.

*Stage 2.* In stage 2, the clinical picture becomes more fixed and apparent. The patient is deeply depressed and apprehensive. Compulsive crying and laughing are present and there may be aimless wandering, repeating certain acts with purposeless hyperactivity. The alterations in speech mechanisms becomes more pronounced with misunderstanding of spoken words, senseless rhyming, automatic repetition of the last words of a sentence. Articulation of words is defective and speech slurred, names mixed up, and sentences contain gross grammatical errors. Reading and writing are seriously impaired. Grand mal epileptic seizures are common in many cases and following the attack there is further marked mental deterioration.

*Stage 3.* In this stage, the patient becomes that of little more than a vegetable and he is deeply demented. Death usually comes from some intercurrent infection.

*Pathology.* Air encephalograms in Alzheimer's disease show diffuse cortical atrophy. Grossly the brain shows a generalized atrophy. Microscopically there is degeneration of nerve cells and senile plaques are quite common.

## Pick's Disease

This disease was first described by A. Pick in a series of papers, the first of which was published in 1892. Pick's disease is a rare condition, being much rarer than Alzheimer's disease. Only about

200 cases have been published in the literature. Women are more frequently affected than men, in proportion of 2:1. Its cause is unknown, although a genetic factor seems to play some part in its occurrence.

The clinical picture is a slowly progressive dementia with aphasia,* aprosexia,** and agnosia.*** There are difficulties in thinking and concentration; the patient is easily fatigued and distractible. Unlike Alzheimer's, memory is not involved. There is a peculiar inability to deal with new problems and situations even though they are quite simple. In the initial stages, emotional changes occur and moral and social values are distorted. As the patient deteriorates intellectually, the symptomatology becomes more characteristic. There is a limitation and slowing down of motor activity, a loss of spontaneity and initiative, and a refusal to talk. Secondly, there is restlessness, talkativeness, and aimless activity. The two modes of behavior are not mutually exclusive; the same patient may exhibit at different times inertia and hyperactivity. Finally, like in Alzheimer's the patient goes into a vegetative existence and there are sporadic epileptiform seizures. The duration of the disease is 2-11 years with an average duration of about 5 years, and it is invariably fatal.

> *Pathology.* There is circumscribed atrophy of both gray and white matter which is localized to one or more lobes of the brain. The localization of the atrophic areas varies from case to case. Microscopic examination of the atrophic areas of the cortex shows a considerable loss of the nerve cells which result in a profound disorganization of the normal cell organization.

## Jackob's Disease

This disease was first described by Jackob and Creutzfeldt in 1921. It occurs primarily between the ages of 45-60. There are three stages to the illness:

> *Stage 1.* Prodromal stage of a few months duration, characterized by slight mental changes such as fatigability, loss of inter-

---

*The loss of the power to use words as symbols of ideas.

**Inability to sustain attention.

***The loss of the ability to recognize familiar objects.

est, memory impairment and episodes of inconsistent behavior.

*Stage 2*. In the second stage, there is a progressive dementia with a narrowing of interests, impairment of memory, intellectual deterioration and apathy. Neurologically, there are tremors and loss of muscle tone.

*Stage 3*. In the final stage, there is extreme dementia, spasticity and motor paralysis.

The course of the disease as contrasted with Pick's and Alzheimer's, is rapid, lasting from 6 months to 2 or 3 years, the average being one year. There is no known cause or cure.

*Pathology*. There are no *gross* changes in the brain of patients suffering from Jackob's disease. However, under the microscope, there is degeneration of the nerve cells of the cerebral cortex spinal cord, and basal ganglia.

## Senile Psychoses and Psychoses with Cerebral Arteriosclerosis

Senile psychoses and psychoses with cerebral arteriosclerosis together constitute the great bulk of serious mental illness in the elderly. They also constitute the great majority of admissions to state mental hospitals. Kolb (14) has estimated that these two psychoses may be expected to show an increase of 200% in the number of first admissions to state mental hospitals by 1980.

The term "senile psychosis" or "senile dementia" are those chronic mental disorders occurring in older individuals which present a variety of clinical pictures which show progressive signs of organic deficit and certain organic characteristic changes in the brain. It is more common in women in the ratio of 2:1 and the onset is usually after 60. There is usually an exaggeration of previous personality traits accompanied by a gradually increasing impairment of efficiency and memory. The gradual deterioration of the brain tissue produces errors in judgement which may have serious repercussions. Deterioration of personal habits and loss of moral inhibitions are early manifestations of the disease; severe untidiness is a later symptom. Insomnia, restlessness, and wandering from home are common. In many cases, there are delusions, hallucinations, and paranoid tendencies. These paranoid tendencies can have unfortunate results since the patient becomes suspicious of the family and he often reverses committments he made to his family. As the psychosis develops, symptoms of intellectual deficit are quite apparent. Immediate memory is seriously impaired and the patient lives in the past indulging in reminiscences about friends and events which happened long ago, though the sequence of events may be seriously altered. Abstract thinking is no longer possible, although the patient retains the ability to perform concrete activities. The psychosis is accompanied by deterioration of the body with a wastage of muscles, shrinkage of soft tissues, and loss of elasticity of the skin. The onset of symptoms until death is 1-11 years.*

> *Pathology.* There is shrinkage of the cerebral cortex and the soft tissue shows marked atrophy. Microscopic examination of the brain reveals atrophy and shrinkage of the nerve cells. The small blood vessels of the brain show thickening and the cerebral cortex shows certain kinds of lesions called senile plaques.

## Arteriosclerotic Psychoses

Arteriosclerotic psychosis includes those mental disorders of elderly people associated with damage that is due to hardening of the cerebral blood vessels. The average age of onset is 66 although the disease may appear in people as young as 45. The symptoms usually have an abrupt onset. Hereditary factors seem to play a significant role although the exact mechanism is not known, and males are more affected than females (3:1) ; the exact reason is not known, but it is possible that hormones play a part. Headache, dizziness, various somatic complaints and physical and mental letdown are common in the initial stages. The onset of the emotional or mental symptoms may be gradual or sudden with about 50% of the cases each way. In those cases where there is a sudden onset, a sudden attack of confusion appears. The patient becomes

---

*An Historical Note.* Since early times, novelists and poets have alluded to senile dementia. Shakespeare's *King Lear* is a good example of a case of senile dementia and Burton's *Anatomy of Melancholy* gives a concise picture of the condition. Jonathan Swift's description of the "Struldberg" in *Gulliver's Travels* is another example; finally P. G. Wodehouse's portrayal of Lord Emsworth depicts the progressive physical and mental failure in senility.

incoherent, restless and quite often hallucinates. He shows a delirious picture which gradually subsides and leaves the patient at a considerably reduced functioning level. During this decline, the intellectual processes, memory and judgment are affected. This defective judgment may affect moral standards. There are also depressive feelings and a fear of impending failure of physical and mental powers.

*Sociological Considerations.* There appears to be high first mental hospital admission rates for cerebral arteriosclerosis in areas of poverty. Gruenberg (15) reported in the city of Syracuse, an area of high first mental hospital admission rates, which had as its ecological characteristics a concentration of multiple family dwellings and a large percentage of people living alone.

*Pathology.* The gross brain picture is one where there are vascular changes and a variety of focal lesions in which the whole cerebral structure is destroyed. The arteries at the base of the brain show characteristic lesions. There may be softening of the brain tissue with anemia and hemorrhaging. Microscopically, there is a thickening of the blood vessels of the brain characteristic of arteriosclerosis. In addition to changes in the brain, there is hardening of the blood vessels of the heart, kidneys and lungs.

## Toxic Delirious Reactions of Old Age

This is a heterogenous group of mental illnesses in which there are distinct metabolic disturbances not only in the brain but of the entire organism. The average age of onset is about 60.

A.*Disorders Due To or Associated with Specific Toxic Agents* Medications and exposure to chemicals may be the causes of acute toxic reactions. Barbiturates and bromide drugs are common causes, as is alcohol.* Delerious toxic reactions are more likely to occur in elderly people who have been confined to

---

*Bailey (M.B.), Haberman, (P.W.), and Alksne (H.), conducted a survey in New York City. The results of this study showed a peak prevalence of alcoholism in the 45-54 group, and 23 per 1000 population aged 20 years and over, a decrease to 17 per 1000 after the age groups of 55-65 a second peak prevalence of 22/1000 at the 65-74 year age group, and a drop to 12 per 1000 for the 75 and over age groups. This was done in the community. Thus, the prevalence of alcoholism as reflected in admissions to psychiatric facilities may not reflect the frequency of alcoholism among the elderly living in a community and not being admitted to a psychiatric facility.

their beds for a long period of time. Acute hallucinations and acute paranoid reactions are prominent symptoms. There are delusions of persecution, apprehension and fear, and suspiciousness may occur beyond the acute stage.

B. *Disorders Due to Trauma*

An acute delerium may follow a head injury with outpouring of blood into the sinuses of the brain. The symptoms are loss of consciousness, followed by amnesia.

C. *Disorders Due to Infection*

Brain infections may arise from local foci; that is, sites of primary infection such as middle ear, and osteomyelitis of the skull. The infection may start in various parts of the body. Infections which affect the meninges (the covering of the brain) come from a number of different bacteria. Viruses can produce encephalitis which is a kind of inflammation of the brain. Of the chronic infections, syphilis is quite common, although with the recent introduction of antibiotics has declined considerably. The symptoms of the delirious intoxications due to infections are a slowing of the mental processes, errors in judgement, and capricious defects in memory. Those affected with syphilis of the brain (general paresis) may have delusions of grandeur.

D. *Alcoholism*

Alcoholism is a major problem in persons aged 45-64. In 1968 alcoholic disorders accounted for 38% of all male admissions in this age group to all types of inpatient psychiatric facilities, varying from 32% in the V.A. Hospitals to 47% in the state and county mental hospitals. In the state hospitals it is the leading admission diagnosis in this age group. In the 65 and over group alcoholism accounted for 12% of all male admissions in 1968 and 11% in 1969. Thus, in 10 years the survivors of the population who are now 55-64 years of age will be 65-74 years old. Thus the possible increase in needs for services for older alcoholics.

## THERAPY AND REHABILITATION

As used in the context of this book, psychotherapy is used in its broadest sense. It includes: the influences of psychodynamic factors on the mental health of the aged, the use of chemical and physical sedation; and somatic therapy as an integrated part of the total therapy and rehabilitation procedures.

**Neuroses**

The attitude of pessimism and indifference which was characteristic of neuroses in later maturity is being replaced by a more hopeful and constructive one. When allowance is made for reduced vigor, agility, and educability in older people, in general with modifications those procedures already in use for treatment of the neuroses in younger people can be made appropriate for older ones. Since elderly people fear invalidism and dependence, these hypochondriacal worries and fears should be dealt with in a firm and constructive manner. In general, in this age group free association techniques are not as efficient as first an analysis of the complaint and utilizing suggestion, advice and explanation, taking into consideration psychodynamic somatic features and constitutional make-up. It is always worth while to try to improve the aging person's health and ameliorating his physical hygiene can be a bridge to establish a meaningful relationship between the therapist and patient. For the patient who continues to work during treatment, it is necessary to evaluate the nature of the work carefully. The patient who cannot work should be given some form of occupational therapy. Occupational therapy serves to distract the patient from painful preoccupations with himself and also provides satisfaction from carrying out various steps in the work itself. Recreation is also an important aspect in the therapeutic milieu of the aged neurotic. The therapist should know what facilities are available in the community. In larger communities, clubs, workshops, guidance clinics have been begun where older men and women can mingle. The therapist should try to adjust the recreational events and interests to his individual needs, interest, and skills.

It is always important in therapy with elderly patients to assess the intrapsychic processes. This applies to all elderly patients, whether or not there are environmental and physical factors affecting their psychopathology. The loss of customary gratifications, without compensation for these gratifications, may lead to feelings of helpless vulnerability, resentment, and anger. the elderly patient may expect further deprivation and punishment. These fears may induce a quest for help, disguised as psychosomatic symptoms. It is the usual *loss* attached to aging that the therapist must understand and accept, as well as the elderly patient's need for dependency and his need to regain a sense of mastery.

The dynamic therapeutic procedures used with the individual neurotic will be very much adjusted to the disorder of the patient. For example, if a memory disorder is present it is of no use to attempt to treat symptoms with extensive dynamic therapy.

When anxiety over sexual matters is the prevailing symptom, direct discussion of these matters may be dangerous and it may be best to talk with such patients about the common sexual problems in his own age group, indicating that this problem is quite common and there are successful solutions. When the complaint of the patient is hypochondriacal, these complaints are treated with objectivity and respect and the patient is assured that he will be studied carefully for the possibility of organic disease. If no organic disease is found, it is helpful to explain that his discomfort is not imaginary, but his sensations are real and distressing. Once the fact is known that no organic pathology does exist, the therapist must stand his ground and not give in to requests for repeated physical examinations. He should state to the patient that treatment will be directed at the underlying emotional disturbance and not the secondary bodily discomforts.

Manipulation of the environment is an extremely important element with older neurotics, especially where children are concerned. Friction may develop over differences in ideas between the generations. Where possible, the older generation should not live with the younger and the need for privacy and comfort should be respected at all times.

An interesting project, which studied the treatment of depression in thirty depressed geriatric residents in two homes for the aged, is described by Power and McCarron*. The treatment group consisted of fifteen residents who each received fifteen weeks of interactive-contact treatment, and fifteen people in a

*Power, Cynthia A. and McCarron, Lawrence T., "Treatment of depression in persons residing in homes for the aged," *The Gerontologist,* 15(2):132-137, April 1975.

control group who continued in their daily routine. The diagnosis of depression was made according to the Brief Psychiatric Rating Scale. In addition to the observational report, the Zung Self Report Depression Scale was completed by each resident.

Interactive-contact treatment consisted of fifteen weeks of half-hour individual sessions; each selected resident was seen for a total of seven and a half hours during the time period. The first phase of treatment concentrated on physical contact and communication between the interviewer and resident. The interviewer began by gently stroking the aged person on his arm, head, and shoulder, in order to establish physical contact. When the interviewer began to respond to the physical communication, verbalized techniques were introduced. For example, the interviewer tried to elicit a physical response by asking the person to do something for him. It was important, once a response was elicited, for the interviewer to continue speaking and being active, and for the patient to not lapse into any strained silence or taking "no" for an answer.

Once this physical-verbal communication was established, the second phase of treatment was begun. This consisted of obtaining resident participation, divided into three phases. The first was to maintain interest and respond to the interviewer. Each session began with a request-response situation (e.g., "Do you remember my name, and how you say it?"). The next phase was to have the resident *do* something with the interviewer. The third part was activating social orientation by introducing others into the experiences (one or two others looking at a picture together). The treatment group had significantly lower scores than the control group, using the Zung Self Report Scale, and there was a significant reduction in depression, as measured by this scale.

In general, intervention strategies with mild emotional disorders of the aged must eliminate many of the stereotyped and obsolete conceptions about such problems. New assumptions concerning aging should include: (1) there is no significant psychological age decrement; (2) society's role functions should be assigned regardless of age; (3) society's resources should be allocated regardless of age; (4) and, sexual behavior is appropriate at all ages, including old age.

One of the best ways to treat the neurotic developments in later life is to prepare people for old age. These people should be encouraged to develop attitudes of acceptance rather than resignation; the latter implies surrender, the former participation. Complete psychological and psychiatric appraisals by competent professional people may be the answer to this problem.

Jonathan A. Barnes, reports an amelioration of behavior when providing "Reality Oriented Therapy" to 6 geriatric patients who exhibited a moderate to severe memory loss, confusion and disorientation. "Reality Oriented Therapy" consists of continually stimulating the patient through repeated presentation of fundamental information and placing him in a group where he competes and meets with other patients and this, according to Barnes, forces him out of isolation. This kind of therapy was instituted 6 days a week for 6 weeks and the changes in the patients' behavior determined by a questionnaire and from observations of the Director of Nurses. A one week follow-up indicated a significant decrease in desirable behavior after this type of therapy was discontinued.

### Psychoneuroses

When the aged person presents a psychoneurotic syndome, he is generally affected in a more drastic way than when the psychoneurosis develops in a younger person. In these cases (contrary to younger people), orthodox psychoanalytic approach is not desirable. Rather, current attitudes and situations should be discussed and what is commonly known as supportive therapy instituted.

### Involutional Psychoses

Hormonal therapy, either with male (androgens) or female (estrogens) hormones has proven to be very helpful in treatment of the involutional psychoses. Electro-convulsive shock therapy has been found to be effective in severely depressed involutional psychotics. One of the advantages of this kind of treatment is that it renders patients who were not previously amenable to psychotherapy, after electric shock makes them accessible to psychotherapy. Electric shock is most useful with those patients in the very severe type of involutional psychoses. The use of metrazol is slightly less effective than electric shock and more dangerous and unpredictable. Occasionally, insulin shock may be used, but is not as effective as metrazol or electric shock.

## The Psychoses

There is no known definitive treatment except custodial for the senile dementias, Alzheimer's Disease, Pick's Disease, or Jackob's Disease.

## Senile Psychoses, Psychoses with Cerebral Arteriosclerosis, and Toxic Delerious Reactions

The main element in treatment of these disorders is supportive and symptomatic. Measures must be taken to protect the patient from harm resulting from bad judgment. Hygienic measures such as proper clothing, adequate diet, bodily cleanliness, etc. are important. Where possible, the patient should be at home where the familiarity of surroundings makes it easy to remain oriented in space since patient will easily develop delirious reactions when removed from their home environment to a hospital. If, because of safety conditions and the advanced state of illness, the patient must be hospitalized, the newer tranquilizers such as serpasil and thorazine have been found to be effective.* Hydrotherapy in the form of continuous baths, electric shock (to combat depression and delusions) and group therapy in cases where there is not too much confusion or depression is indicated. In patients with psychoses with arteriosclerosis, activities which throw great strain on the heart should be avoided.

Senile patients with marked physical disabilities develop a "mixed bag" of psychological reactions ranging from the most common responses of regression, depression, psychoneurosis and psychosis as a reaction to these disabilities.

Wittich and Enke-Ferchland (1968) (Wittich, G, Enke-Ferchland, E.—Mehydimension ale intergrierte gruppen therapie

*70% of all patients in long term care are on psychoactive drugs.

in der psychosomatischen rehabilitation—Psychotherapy and Psychosomatics, (1968, 16, 261-270) reported that group therapy with patients with cardiac disease and ulcerative colitis resulted in amelioration of symptoms. Bellak and Small (1965) (Bellak L., and Small, L.—Emergency psychotherapy and brief psychotherapy—New York, Grune Stratton, 1965) and Parfitt (1967) (Parfitt, H.L.—Psychiatric Aspects of Regional Enteritis—Canadian Medical Association Journal, 1967, 97, 807-811) also report case histories where psychotherapy facilitated the patient's response to medical treatment. Kurasik (1967) (Kurasik, S.—Group Dynamics in The Rehabilitation of Hemiplegic Patients —Journal of American Geriatric Society, 1967, 15, 852-855) treated 15 hemiplegic patients whose hemiplegia was due to cerebral thrombosis, some with individual and some with group therapy for ten weeks. He found that the hemiplegics in group therapy reached the maximum goals set by the staff 8 days before the patients treated by individual therapy. Godbole, and Verinis (Godbole, Anil and Verinis, S. Scott—Physically III Geriatric Patients—The Gerontologist, 14, 2, April 1974 pp. 143-148) report the results of brief psychotherapy with 61 aged patients (average age 69 yrs.) who had a variety of physical disorders including cardiovascular, neurological, musculoskeletal, and a miscellaneous group. One group (N-20) received brief psychotherapy with a confrontation statement. This is a psychotherapeutic technique developed by Garner (Garner, H.H. Psychotherapy Applied To Comprehensive Medical Practice—Illinois Medical Journal, 1969, 135, 289-295) known as the confrontation problem solving technique which include the presentation of statements dealing with conflicts to a maladaptive behavior pattern. For example, a statement such as "Stop believing you will never leave the hospital," is followed at an appropriate time with "What do you think about what I told you," requiring the continued exploration of this statement, possibilities of new learning attitudes and the gaining of insight.

The second group (N-19) received brief psychotherapy without a confrontation statement and the third group received two evaluation interviews, but no formal psychotherapy, Nurses ratings, therapist's ratings, doctor's ratings, patient's measures

(ZUNG Depression Scale and a measure of self-concept) and discharge were the criteria of improvement. In general the first group were more improved than the other groups and the "confrontation problem solving" technique was found to be the most effective of the two psychotherapy techniques.

## The Mentally Retarded

Since idiots and imbeciles (I.Q. Score 30-60) on the average die early, it would be expected that seniles who in youth score in the dull-normal category would constitute the majority of the aged subnormal; this has been found to be the case.

There are great practical difficulties which impede the accurate measurement of intelligence in the aged mentally retarded. In addition to the problem of enforced individual assessment of their intelligence, there is the one of advanced age and the difficulties of assessment* in the aged. Organic deterioration is quite common in aged idiots and imbeciles, although much more common in certain clinical types than others. For example, deterioration is present at all age levels in Mongoloid deficiency including cortical atrophy and hemorrhaging of the spinal cord and brain.

## Adjustment of Older Subnormals

Age presents a blessing and a curse with the subnormal. On the one hand, the lifetime of experience behind them have enabled the elderly subnormal to come to grips with their environment and many have found a niche particularly in the labor market and where their talents can be utilized. On the other hand, age with all its difficulties adds to an already severe handicap.

Older defectives who are institutionalized frequently are more fortunate than normals of the same age group and many such defectives do not want to exchange their security for the freedom of life outside an institution.

It is not difficult usually to differentiate between psychotic seniles and older defectives without psychosis. The differentiation between senile psychotics without mental deficiency and senile psychotics with mental deficiency can usually be made by means of

---

*See pp. 46, 47, supra.

past history such as for example a record of institutionalization in an institution for the mentally retarded and such records as ones dealing with occupation, employment, and education.

In general, knowledge concerning the aged subnormal is quite sketchy at this time. For example almost nothing is known about the sensory and psychomotor functions of the aged subnormal and the effect of age on criminality, suicide, and sexuality in the subnormal.

## Hospitalization of the Aged Mentally Ill

Up till very recently, the aged mentally ill spent their declining years in mental hospitals, primarily in state mental hospitals.* For the majority of patients in years gone by, mental hospitals provided very little specific treatment but only custodial care, protection and a certain way of life. In the more modern hospital, this has radically changed. Examples of this can be obtained from a description of a study by Hanfman (16) who made a study of the evaluation of 46 (30 men and 16 women) patients in a state hospital of their lives in the hospitals. Two-thirds of the group were schizophrenic, half of these of the paranoid type. The remainder belonged to various diagnostic categories. The results were obtained by means of a special "disguised" interview technique in order to obviate the tendency of patients to give "correct" or "good" answers. To supplement the material obtained, case tory records were reviewed and ward behavior observed. Hanfman found that 35% of the patients studied are acutely unhappy; 13% are not happy but resigned to their fate and 52% obtain satisfaction from their lives which make it worth living. In 39% of the cases, experiences and attitudes rooted in the disease are foremost in determining the happiness or discontent; in 48% of the cases, the patient's satisfaction or dissatisfaction depends primarily on situational factors, i.e., the strengths and weaknesses of institutional life.

The practical application of these findings are that the mental hospital is a place for treatment and cure and as such a transition-

*There has been a decrease of about 150,000 geriatric patients in the last five years in state mental hospitals.

al place for the patient who desires to leave the hospital. However, when treatment fails, the mental hospital takes on the function of a domicile for custodial care. Since most modern mental hospitals center their treatment on facilities for recently admitted patients because they are the most hopeful in terms of prognosis, the older patient (in both chronological terms and stay at the hospital) is neglected with a consequent therapeutic loss. More prolonged and therapeutic efforts in this regard with these older patients might lead to discharge before they became too old or lost contact with reality.

A step in this direction has been taken in a hospital where the author was a part-time staff member.

In 1959, an effort was made to intensify treatment of elderly patients at Napa State Hospital in the North San Francisco Bay Region in Northern California (17). From the beginning, emphasis was placed on social service and maintaining active relationships with relatives and close friends with the ultimate goal of returning the improved patients to their own community. Treatment was instituted as soon as these patients were on the wards. Four steps were instituted.

a) Building a one-to-one relationship. Each patient was assigned to a staff member (usually a psychiatric technician) who offered guidance and support and established "movement" toward therapy.

b) After this initial step, a second patient is introduced as a kind of "buddy" to the first patient. The second patient is a "weaker" individual with more needs whom the original patient can help, thus coming to feel needed. When the original patient accepts responsibility for the care of the new patient, he is ready for the next step.

c) Group therapy is then instituted — usually patients in groups of 4-8 for resocialization and remotivation.

d) Gradual reintegration into the community by arranging for shopping trips, parties, church activities, picnics, senior citizen's clubs, etc. These are primarily entertainment not therapy sessions.

When the deterioration of the patient is still in the reversible stage, changes take place quickly and the patient is often ready to return to the community in 4-6 weeks. Up to the present time, 41% of the women and 29% of the men admitted have been released within one year after admission. Extrapolating for the future, Todd predicts that 4 of every 10 elderly patients will be released from the hospital. There is also a low return rate among these elderly patients.

This kind of program is now the trend in many state mental hospitals and mental hospitals in general can follow the example of Napa State Hospital.

In the hospitalization of aged psychiatric patients, the question comes up whether to place these patients on wards with their age peers or intersperse them with patients of all ages. While a great deal of research has been done with age segregated housing for normal elderly and retired persons,* there has been only one study on the effects of age segregation on interaction patterns of aged psychiatric patients (18). At the Medical Care Research Center at the University of Washington, 55 consecutive male admissions to a state psychiatric hospital were randomly assigned to one of three study wards — to an age segregated custodial ward, to an age heterogeneous custodial ward and to a therapy ward. Methods of interaction were measured by actual observations of patient behavior, staff ratings of patient behavior, a semi-structured interview which measured attitudes, and a projective measure of interaction provided by responses to a specially constructed TAT card.

The general results of this study were that elderly patients show more interaction in an age heterogeneous environment than age segregated environments. These findings are at variance with the studies on non-institutional groups which report more interaction by elderly people in segregated settings. The results of this study seem to upset the notion that behavior settings with a high concentration of aged patients allow greater opportunity for leadership and greater "penetrance" for the aged. The reason is

---

*See Geist, H.: *The Psychological Aspects of Retirement,* C. C. Thomas, Springfield, Illinois, 1968, pp. 102-109.

probably that the aged psychiatric population do not have the psychological resources necessary to take advantage of leadership opportunities.

## BIBLIOGRAPHY

1. Dunham, H. Warren: Sociological aspects of mental disorders in later life. In: Kaplan, Oscar J. (ed.) : *Mental Disorders in Later Life*, 2nd ed. Stanford, California, Stanford University Press, 1956, p. 169.
2. Belknap, I., and Friedsam, H. J.: Age and sex categories as sociological variables in the mental disorders of later maturity. *Am. Sociol. Rev., 14*:367-76, 1949.
3. Giese, F.: Erlebnesformen des Alters — Umfrageergebnisse Über Merk-marle Personalischen Verfalls. *Deutsch. Psychol. 5*, No. 2, Halle Markold, 1928.
4. Jones, L. W.: Personality and age. *Nature* (London) , *136*:779-82, 1935.
5. Landis, J. T.: What is the happiest period in life? *School and Society, 55*: 643-645, 1942.
6. Kuhlen, R. G.: Age differences in personality during adult years. *Psychol. Bull., 42*:333-358, 1945.
7. Hamilton, G. V.: Changes in personality and psychosexual phenomena. Chapter 30 in Cowdry, E. V. (ed.) : *Problems of Aging*, 2nd ed. Baltimore, Williams and Wilkins, 1942, pp. 810-831.
8. Hentig, H. V.: *Crime: Causes and Conditions*. New York, McGraw-Hill Book Co., 1947, pp. 151-155.
9. Hamilton, G.: Changes in personality and psychosexual phenomena with age. In: Cowdry, E. V.: *Problems of Aging*, 2nd ed. Baltimore, Williams and Wilkins, 1942, pp. 254-301.
10. Baker, Marcella, and Wilensky, Harold: Fantasy and Adjustment in the Older Adult. Paper Delivered before Annual Meeting of the American Psychological Association, New York City, September, 1966.
11. Kutner, B., Fanshel, D., Togo, A. M., and Langner, T. S.: *Five Hundred Over 60*. New York, Russell Sage Foundation, 1956.
12. Busse, E. W., Barnes, R. H., and Dovenmuehle, R. H.: The Incidence and Origins of Hypochondriacal Patterns and Psychophysiological Reactions in Elderly Persons. First Pan-American Congress of Gerontology, Mexico City, Sept. 1956.
13. Walters, T., and Woltman, H.: Nervous and mental aspects of old age. *New Orleans M. & S. J., 93*:187-93, 1940.
14. Kolb, L.: The Psychiatric Significance of Aging as a Public Health Problem. Supplement 168 to U. S. Public Health Reports, U. S. Government Printing Office, 1942 .
15. Gruenberg, E. M.: Community Conditions and Psychoses of the Elderly. *Am. J. Psychiatry, 110*:888-896, 1954.

16. Hanfman, Eugenia: Older mental patients after long hospitalization. In: Kaplan, O. J.: *Mental Disorders in Later Life.* Stanford, Calif., Stanford U. Press, 1956, pp. 352-382.

17. Todd, Ramona: Fate of elderly patients in an intensive therapy program of a state mental hospital. *The Journal-Lancet, 86:*No. 4, 201-203, April, 1966; and Todd, Ramona: Early treatment reverses symptoms of senility. *Hospital and Community Psychiatry,* June, 1966, 170-171.

18. Kahana, Eva: The Effects of Age Segregation on Interaction Patterns of Aged Psychiatric Patients. Paper read at the American Psychological Association Meeting, Sept. 5, 1967.

19. Back, K.: Transitions to Age and Self-Image, Normal Aging II. *Reports from Duke Longitudinal Studies,* 1970-73, edited by Palmore, E., Duke University Press, 1974, 207-216, by permission.

20. Pfeiffer, E., Verwoerdt, A., and Davis, G.C.: Sexual Behavior in Middle Life, Normal Aging II. *Reports from Duke Longitudinal Studies,* 1970-73, edited by Palmore, E., Duke University Press, 1974, 243-251, by permission.

21. Graney, M.A.: Happiness and Social Participation in Aging. *Journal of Gerontology, 30:*106, 701-706, 1965.

22. Busse, E.W., and Wang, H.S.: The Multiple Factors Contributing to Dementia in Old Age, Normal Aging II. *Reports from Duke Longitudinal Studies,* 1970-73, edited by Palmore, E., Duke University Press, 1974, 153-160, by permission.

23. Bailey, M.B., Haberman, P.W., and Alksne, H.: The Epidemiology of Alcoholism in an Urban Residential Area. *Quarterly Journal of Studies of Alcohol, 26:*19-40, 1965.

24. Wittich, G., Enke-Ferchiand, E.: Mehrdimension als Intergrierte Gruppen Therapie in der Psychosomatischen Rehabilitation. *Psychotherapy and Psychosomatics, 16:*261-270, 1968.

25. Bellak, L., and Small, L.: *Emergency Psychotherapy and Brief Psychotherapy,* New York, Grune Stratton, 1965.

26. Parfitt, H.L.: Psychiatric Aspects of Regional Enteritis. *Canadian Medical Association Journal,* 1967, *97:*807-811, 1967.

27. Kurasik, S.: Group Dynamics in the Rehabilitation of Hemiplegic Patients. *Journal of the American Geriatric Society, 15:*852-855, 1967.

28. Codbole, A., and Verinis, S.S.: Brief Psychotherapy in the Treatment of Emotional Disorders in Physically Ill Geriatric Patients. *The Gerontologist, 14:*2, 143-148, April, 1974.

29. Garner, H.H.: Psychotherapy Applied to Comprehensive Medical Practice. *Illinois Medical Journal, 135:*289-295, 1969.

30. Power, C.A., and McCarron, L.T.: Treatment of Depression in Persons Residing in Homes for the Aged. *The Gerontologist, 15:*2, 132-137, April, 1975.

31. Cleveland, Wm. P., and Gianturco, D.T.: Remarriage Probability after Widowhood; A Retrospective Method. *Journal of Gerontology, 1:*31, 99-103, January, 1976.

## General References

1. Busse, E. W.: Psychopathology. In Birren, J. E. (ed.) : *Handbook of Aging in the Individual.* Chicago, U. of Chicago Press, 1959, pp. 364-399.
2. Cameron, Norman: Neuroses of later life. In Kaplan, O. J. (ed.) : *Mental Disorders of Later Life.* Stanford, Calif., Stanford Univ. Press, 1956, pp. 201-243.
3. Cavan, Ruth S.: *Criminology.* New York, Thomas Y. Crowell Company, 1962.
4. Corsellis, J. A. N.: *Mental Illness and the Aging Brain.* London, Oxford University Press, 1962.
5. Dovenmuehle, R. H., and Verwoerdt, H.: Physical and depressive symptoms in hospitalized cardiac patients. *J. Amer. Geriatric Soc., 10:* 932-947, 1962.
6. Glaser, D., and Rice, K.: Crime, age and employment. In: Wolfgang, M. E., Savitz, L., and Johnson, N. (eds.) : *The Sociology of Crime and Delinquency.* New York, John Wiley and Sons, 1962, pp. 163-169.
7. Goldhammer, E. H., Cavan, Ruth, Burgess, E. W., and Havighurst, R. J.: *Personal Adjustments in Old Age.* Chicago, Science Research Associates, 1949.
8. Hamilton, G. V.: Changes in personality and psychosexual phenomena. Chapter 30 in Cowdry, E. V. (ed.) : *Problems of Aging,* 2nd ed. Baltimore, Williams and Wilkins, 1942, pp. 810-831.
9. Himler, L. E., and Morrisey, V.: Factors influencing prognosis in psychiatric illness of the aged. *J. Amer. Geriatrics Soc., 3:*811-816, 1955.
10. Hoch, P. H., and Zubin, S. (eds.) : *Psychopathology of Aging.* New York, Grune and Stratton Inc., 1961.
11. Hollingshead, A. B., and Redlich, F. C.: *Social Class and Mental Illness.* New York, John Wiley and Sons, 1958.
12. Jelliffe, J. E., and White, W. A.: *Diseases of the Nervous System,* 5th ed.: Philadelphia, Lea and Febiger, 1929.
13. Kaplan, O. J.: *Mental Disorders of Later Life.* Stanford, Calif., Stanford Univ. Press, 1956.
14. Kaufman, M.: Old age and aging: The psychoanalytic view. *Am. J. Orthopsychiat., 10:*73-79, 1940.
15. Obrist, W. D., Busse, E. W., Eisdorfer, C., and Kleemeier, R. W.: Relation of the electroencephalogram to intellectual function in senescence. *J. Geront., 17:*197-206, 1962.
16. O'Neal, Patricia, Robin, E., and Schmidt, E. H.: A psychiatric study of attempted suicide in persons over sixty years of age. *Arch. Neurol. and Psychiat., 75:*275-284, 1956.
17. Post, F.: *The Significance of Affective Symptoms in Old Age.* London, Oxford Univ. Press, 1962.
18. Reichard, Suzanne, Livson, N., and Petersen, P. G.: *Aging and Personality.* New York, John Wiley and Sons, Inc., 1962.

19. Stieglitz, E. J. (ed.) : *Geriatric Medicine,* 3rd ed. Philadelphia, E. B. Lippincott Co.
20. Zinberg, N. W., and Kaufman, I. (eds.) : *Normal Psychology of the Aging Process.* New York, International Universities Press Inc., 1963.

# Chapter V

# RESEARCH AND AGING

THIS CHAPTER will be devoted to research on aging and the facilities now extant for such research as well as possibilities for future research in this field.

Research in gerontology extends from the investigation of fundamental problems in biology through the physiological, mental and personality characteristics of humans to the large economic factors associated with aging. The primary purpose of research on aging is to characterize the nature of the older organism and to explain how the organism changes over time.

There are various ways of studying the aging process in terms of the kinds of studies done. These are:

1) Studies on longevity which are dependent on a variety of variables such as genetic background, parental age, nutrition, and cultural differences, etc. These studies may be cross sectional, that is, over a short period of time, or longitudinal, over a long period of time. The best method is the longitudinal, but for administrative and practical reasons, these kinds of studies cannot always be done. Some of these studies have already been discussed in previous sections of the text.

2) Another kind of study is concerned with differences with age in a range of biological, psychological and social characteristics and the study of age differences in particular characteristics. Included in such studies are those done on lower animals. We can more easily examine tissues, cells, and cellular components because they have a relatively short life span and can be subjected to a wide range of changes in diet and environmental conditions. Sometimes, psychological variables can be studied more easily in lower animals.

135

3) A third type of study concerns the historical aspects of the experience of an individual or group. Quite often, hypotheses derived from biographical and historical studies can be tested in predicted longitudinal studies. These studies concentrate on those biological and psychological aspects which are part of the organism or characteristic of him in comparison with the group or norm, and which of his patterns remain unique or distinctive of him over his life span.

Research designs in the aged may be classified as two essential types:

1) *Representative Design.* In representative design, the research investigator studies the aging process in representative or typical subjects and "representative" environments in order to make generalizations about processes and relationships as they occur.
2) *Experimental Design.* In experimental design, the investigator extracts a process from its natural context and places it in a controlled or experimental context.

Research in aging is often a combination of both types of design.

The past decade has seen a marked impetus to research in gerontology. During that time, there has not only been a marked increase in the total number of articles published on old age,* but there has been a remarkable increase in the number of experimental studies on the aging process, both in the medical and behavioral sciences.

Since the biological and psychological aspects of the aging process are closely connected, both aspects of past, ongoing, and potentialities for future research will be discussed.

## BIOLOGICAL ASPECTS

Comfort (1) has published a summary of research on the biological aspects of aging.

Genetic influences have been shown to be a powerful factor

---

*It has been estimated that in the past decade there have been as many studies published on old age as in the previous 50 years.

in the aging process. A number of experiments with strains of fruit flies have shown clearly that widely different life spans could be isolated by selective breeding. Matings between long lived mice have shown that longevity is a characteristic that is determined by parental influences. Kallman's studies on twins show that similar factors operate in humans (2).

Shortening of the life span by overfeeding has been demonstrated in silkworms and small aquatic animals. McCoy has shown that caloric restriction in rats significantly extends the life span. A number of investigators have studied the activity of specific enzymes in tissues from animals of various ages. Most of this work has been done on the rat and guinea pig, but additional studies have been performed on blood vessels removed from human autopsy. These studies show that the rate of utilization of oxygen is slower in old than in young tissues. Certain physiological functions do not change with age or change very little, e.g., there is little evidence for changes in the pH of the blood, the sugar content of the blood, or the total volume of the blood present in the body with advancing age. However, in the study of specific bodily organs with aging, the amount of blood perfusing through the kidney decreases from the age of 30 upward. Similarly, recent research on the maximum amount of air expired from the lungs, maximum amount of air that can be moved through the lungs, the amount of blood pumped by the heart, excretion of certain hormones, and the conduction of nerve impulses in the peripheral nerve show a gradual decrease with age. Many new developments in surgery and medicine have been made in the last 10 years in gerontology. Practically every medical school and teaching hospital in the United States is engaged in some research associated with various diseases of old age. New developments in surgery permit grafting of new blood vessels. Advances in endocrinology show that older people benefit from the supervised administration of the male and female sex hormones. The introduction of cortisone and ACTH has mitigated the suffering of older arthritis patients. The discovery of antibiotics has greatly reduced the mortality of infectious diseases in the aged.

## PSYCHOLOGICAL AND SOCIOLOGICAL
## ASPECTS OF AGING

Many of the research studies on the psychological aspects of aging have been reviewed above. Some of the more pertinent recent advances will be summarized here. Perhaps the outstanding gross generalization is that speed of performance diminishes with age, and this speed decrement also varies with the complexity of the task and in newly learned performance. There are age decrements in perception and sensory processes, but these are not as limiting as one might think because of various sensory aids such as glasses, hearing aids, etc. Decrements in intelligence with advancing age are not as great as originally thought and much of the decrement can be attributed to limitations in educational background, decreased motivation in the testing process, and decreased sensory awareness, important in speed tests. In the field of learning, acquisition of a new skill is slower because of motivation factors and interference from previously learned materials. The maintenance of interests and a large spectrum of activities are the best insurance against maladjustment.

Sociological research has gone hand in hand with biological and physiological. Various questionnaires and surveys have been conducted in cities and rural areas which shed light on urbanization of the elderly and to what extent older people want to participate in community life. The distribution of older people in the population, their places of residence and migration studies, indicated interesting mobility trends among the elderly.*

## CURRENT FACILITIES FOR RESEARCH ON AGING

This section will enable the student to have a reference guide to current facilities for the study of the aged.

## FEDERAL AGENCIES

The National Institutes of Health and the National Institute of Mental Health both have gerontology units. The Unit on Gerontology of the National Institutes of Health was established

---

*See pp. 12-15, supra.

as part of the Division of Physiology in 1940. With the establishment of the National Heart Institute in 1948, the gerontology section was transferred to this Institute and currently functions as one of the operating units of the Intramural Research Division of the National Heart Institute. The Baltimore City Hospitals work in a close administrative and functioning capacity with the Federal institutes in providing patients and research facilities for the study of gerontology.

In 1951, the National Institute of Mental Health established a section on aging and in 1956, this Institute joined with the Heart Institute in providing a program on the psychological aspects of aging. The overall research goals of the combined Gerontology Branch include:

a) A comprehensive study of the medical and physiological processes in aging.
b) Experimental investigation of personality, mental performance, and emotional and social characteristics of the aged.

In 1974, as the result of an act of Congress, a National Institute of Aging was set up. As of the first revision of this book, the National Institute of Aging has a permanent director by the name of Doctor Robert Butler, a highly respected geriatric psychiatrist.

In 1975 a new Center for the Studies of the Mental Health of the Aging was set up at the National Institute of Mental Health, as part of the Institute's Division of Special Mental Health Programs. Chief of the Center is a psychiatrist, Eugene Cohen. The research programs will be conducted by psychologist Thomas Anderson. This Center will act as the central point within the National Institute of Mental Health for the Development, coordination, and evaluation of research, training, and services related to the mental health of the elderly. Active collaboration is also planned within the Department of Health, Education, and Welfare; other agencies, both government and non-government are concerned with programs for the aged.

## UNIVERSITIES AND MEDICAL SCHOOLS

1) *Washington University and Medical School* in St. Louis operates an interdisciplinary research program in gerontology under the general supervision of the Division of Gerontology which is part of the medical school. The departments of psychology, psychiatry, anatomy, and adult education of the University all cooperate by contributing both staff members and facilities for ongoing research in gerontology. In addition, the laboratories and facilities of the St. Louis City Hospitals, the Jewish Hospital, the Chronic Hospital, and the Old People's Home in St. Louis contribute greatly to ongoing studies. One of the unique contributions of this program is the acceptance of young investigators from outside the United States who work and study for a period of one or two years in research, and exchange of information from the country from whence they came.

2) *Institute of Gerontology, University of Florida, Gainesville, Florida.*

Most of the research conducted by this Institute concerns the sociological aspects of aging. Because of the large number of elderly people residing in Florida, the State of Florida provides a fertile ground for such research. Studies of communities, living arrangements and migration of the elderly have been carried out within certain departments of the University.

3) *Institute of Gerontology, State University of Iowa,* Iowa City, Iowa.

This Institute has two main functions:

1) To supply information and competent· advice to communities engaged in building programs for the aged.
2) To organize discussion groups, support of personnel, and to engage in research in gerontology. In addition, members of the Institute lecture to various colleges and departments of the university such as the medical school, school of liberal arts, commerce and social work courses. A monthly bulletin is published by the Institute on various aspects of the aging process.

4) *Division of Gerontology, Institute of Human Relations, University of Michigan,* Ann Arbor, Michigan.

The Division of Gerontology of the Institute of Human Relations of the University of Michigan was established in 1951. Annual conferences are held which have served a useful function in emphasizing various aspects of aging such as action programs and research follow up of these programs. The Division has also conducted surveys of communities and recreational programs for institutions for the aged. The first course in pre-retirement education in the United States was developed at the University of Michigan and because of contacts of the University with industry throughout the state, pre-retirement counseling instruction has been given in these courses. In 1966, Wayne State University's Board of Governors and the Regents of the University of Michigan approved the establishment of a jointly operated Institute of Gerontology to explore more fully the whole gamut of problems of the science of gerontology.

5) *Institute of Gerontology, University of Miami*, Miami, Florida.

The Institute of Gerontology was established at the University of Miami and is primarily interested in research and training on the medical problems, diseases, and rehabilitation of older people.

6) *Department of Gerontology, University of Kansas Medical School*, Kansas City, Kansas.

This department is concerned with clinical research on aged patients and offers post graduate courses to physicians on medical problems in gerontology.

7) *College of Physicians and Surgeons, Columbia University*, New York City.

In the area of psychobiology, studies on aging in twins have revealed similarities in the nature of both physical and behavioral disease processes in aging twins. In addition to research on humans, research on animals is continuing at the College of Physicians and Surgeons with autopsy studies on animals who have been subjected to precise environmental conditions such as air conditioning, uniform lighting, etc.

8) *Cornell University*, Ithaca, New York.

Longitudinal studies on dogs in the College of Agriculture at Cornell University and studies on diet, influence of exercise, and nutritional requirements of animals with advancing age have been studied. Here also the surgical grafting of two animals has made possible the studies of artificial Siamese twins with the production of pairs of animals who differed as much as a year in age. The question being studied is whether attachments of such animals results in the rejuvenation of the older member of the pair or more rapid senescence in the younger.

9) *University of Minnesota,* Minneapolis, Minnesota.

In the Department of Physiological Hygiene at the University of Minnesota, important longitudinal studies are going on with white collar workers and railroad workers. Certain physical and anthropometric measurements are made on white collar workers and they are also given psychological tests and a questionnaire on diet and physical activity. Impending cardio-vascular disease can be predicted from certain measurements. The health status of physically active railroad yard workers have been compared with sedentary workers over long periods of time.

10) *University of Chicago,* Chicago, Illinois.

The Committee on Human Development of the University of Chicago has an ongoing interest on the sociological aspects of the aging process. They have analyzed the meaning of work to older people and retirement. Cooperative studies between the Committee on Human Development, the Institute of Industrial Relations, the Department of Psychology, and the National Opinion Research Center have yielded a great deal of worth while information on the aging process.

11) *University of Louisville,* Louisville, Kentucky.

One of the few colonies of aged guinea pigs in the United States has been raised at the University of Louisville, in Louisville, Kentucky. Here, studies are being done on changes in various organs and blood chemistry with age. Researchers have been able to lengthen the life span of the guinea pigs at this laboratory some six years beyond that of the average life span of a guinea pig.

12) *Duke University,* Durham, North Carolina.

The Council of Gerontology at Duke University, involving many university disciplines is encouraging interdisciplinary research on aging in order to expand knowledge in the field by securing funds for research, education, publications, and various kinds of scholarships and fellowships.

13) *Purdue University,* Lafayette, Indiana.

The Department of Adult Education has organized a community study involving the psychological and sociological aspects of aging of individuals living in the community. These studies are primarily concerned with the factors that determine attitudes of older people towards aging in the community and the factors that determine community attitudes toward aging people.

14) *University of Southern California,* Los Angeles.

A program to train specialists from the fields of architecture, psychology, social work, biology, sociology, education, economics, and physical education to take over national leadership in research and teaching in gerontology has begun at the Research on Adult Development and Aging Institute at the University of Southern California. The program is being financed under five-year grants from the United States Public Health Service with full tuition scholarships and grants given to trainees, the amount depending on the trainee's previous academic work.

In 1967, grants were awarded by the Federal government under Title V of the Older Americans Act to various colleges and universities for the purpose of expanding education about and expansion of knowledge concerning the aging process and retirement.

A grant was given to Teachers College, Columbia University to provide education in planning and directing recreation programs for older persons, planning and administration of multipurpose centers and teaching and research in the field of recreation and aging. The Institute of Aging of the University of South Florida in Tampa has received a substantial grant to study the educational needs of specialists in the field of aging. The Graduate Center for the Study of Gerontology at the University of Oregon at Eugene received a substantial stipend to expand a research program on biological, behavioral and social phenomena of aging and initiate a teaching program to prepare qualified people to serve the older population of the Western United States. As the result of a government grant, the University of Georgia Graduate School of Business Administration has set up short term educational programs for retirement housing personnel. The San Diego State College Foundation has received a grant to provide graduate training at the School of Social Work at that College to study community planning and organization of services for older people. The Florence Heller School of Advanced Studies in Social Welfare at Brandeis University has received a grant to develop specialists in social gerontology.

## PRIVATE INSTITUTIONS AND INSTITUTES

1) *Fels Institute,* Yellow Springs, Ohio.

The Fels Institute has been carrying on longitudinal studies among children and their parents involving several generations. The measurements include primarily those on growth and development, more specifically chemical alterations in body composition and personality characteristics.

2) *Creedmore Institute for Psycho-Biologic Studies,* Queens Village, New York.

Studies are being conducted at this Institute on the relationship between the physiological and psychological aspects of aging.

3) *Age Center of New England,* Boston, Massachusetts.

The Age Center of New England has organized a program for pre-retirement training, counseling and recreational activities of older people. The Center is supported by funds from industry in the Boston area and one of the aims of the Center is to ascertain measures which will help business and industry to deal more effectively with preretired and retired workers.

4) *Hospitals and Homes for the Aged in New York City.*

Several of the hospitals in New York City have devoted themselves primarily to the problem of the study of the aged, principally the medical aspects.

   a) *Goldwater Memorial Hospital,* Welfare Island, New York City. Changes in body composition with age and studies on the rehabilitation of older patients are being studied at this hospital. Here, training is given to physicians in the medical, psychiatric, and sociological aspects of patients with chronic diseases.

b) *Brooklyn Home and Hospital for the Aged and Infirm Hebrews,* Brooklyn, New York. At this hospital, clinical research studies are in progress on the diseases of old age with specific emphasis on rheumatoid arthritis, arteriosclerosis, and endocrine diseases.

c) *Home for Aged and Infirm Hebrews,* New York City. A unique contribution of this home is the rehabilitation program for elderly hemiplegics and research on the activity programs of various kinds on the social adjustment in the aged. Research is also going on concerning age changes in carbohydrate metabolism and on the structural changes of the eye with aging.

d) *Home and Hospital for the Daughters of Jacob,* New York City. At this hospital, research is being conducted on nutrition and the effects of vitamin supplements on the aged.

Shock has envisioned an Institute of Gerontology with specific emphasis on research in all areas of the aging, educating both older and younger workers in the field, instruction for the aged to prepare them for the exigencies of this period of life, educating communities in regard to the usefulness and capacities of elderly people, and the rehabilitation and care of elderly people. The closest that such an institute has come to fruition is the newly established one at the University of Southern California with Doctor James Birren as its head.

## FUTURE RESEARCH

Future research will center both on animal and human experimentation. Problems in genetics, the physical and chemical properties of protoplasm, biochemistry, physiology, histology, pathology, and various behavioral characteristics in both animals and humans should be investigated. These will require long term and repeated observations beginning perhaps with the age of 15 and continuing throughout the life span of the individual. The cooperation of normally productive aged people in the community with researchers will be needed. In addition to the studies on the functional capacities of different organs systems and their interrelations, provisions must be made for various criteria for all around performance of various organ systems with adequate measures of the rate of response and recovery. This will require the cooperation of scientists from many disciplines — physiology, biochemistry, and the behavioral sciences. The solution of socioeconomic problems with the aged must go hand in hand with the research in the physical and behavioral sciences. For example, such problems as medical care and medical costs, training programs to rehabilitate older workers, development of programs for community services for older and retired people, and employment and living arrangements best adapted to old age should be investigated.

## RESEARCH ON THE AGED IN FOREIGN COUNTRIES

### Great Britain

At the Whittington Hospital in London, Doctor V. Korenchevsky has done a great deal of work on the endocrine aspects of aging particularly in the rat.

At St. John's Hospital in London, Dr. T. H. Howell, in charge of medical services, is carrying on an extensive research program on aging in arteries and diseases of the joints.

Dr. Bourne of the London Hospital Medical College is investigating age changes in the structural characteristics of various tissues using various cytological and histological techniques.

Lord Amulree at St. Pancras Hospital is developing an effective rehabilitation program whereby elderly bedridden patients with adequate nursing and medical care, can lead successful and happy lives under domiciliary care or in private homes.

At the universities in England, much work is going on in research on the aged. At Cambridge, Doctor McCance has studied the responses of old and young men to starvation. Doctor Welford has done a great deal of research on the psychological aspects of aging, where emphasis is placed on the measurement and analysis of human skills and the effectiveness of retraining programs for industrial placement. E. C. Fleming at the Department of Industrial Medicine at the University of Sheffield has conducted important surveys of the age structure of workers in a variety of industries in Great Britain. At the University of Liverpool, Dr. D. B. Bromley has investigated the effects of age on creative intellectual output. Dr. Comfort of the Department of Zoology of the University of London is attempting to study the effects of parental age on longevity. Doctor T. H. Howell, chief of medicine at St. John's Hospital in London has pioneered in developing "Half Way Houses" where nursing services were established which permitted care of patients not ill enough to occupy beds in the acute hospital but still unable to care for themselves at home or in boarding homes.

### France

Doctor F. Bourliére of the Faculty of Medicine at the University of Paris has made arrangements with various manufacturing firms whereby workers between the ages of 20-65 as well as older retirees come to the geriatric research unit at the School of Medicine for a series of psychological and physiological tests at annual intervals.

### Denmark

Doctor Torbin Geill* who is chief of Old People's Town in Copenhagen, Denmark has, in addition to administering this interesting institution, investigated many clinical problems in elderly patients particularly in the area of nutrition, cardiovascular, and blood physiology. Doctor C. Hamburger of the State Serum Institute in Copenhagen, Denmark, has instituted interesting research on the excretion of various hormones in older people.

### Finland

At the University of Helsinki, studies are going on under the direction of Doctor Eeva Jalavisto of the effects of parental age on longevity. Jalavisto has analyzed the geneological records from many of Scandinavia's noble families. The work of Doctor Jalavisto is being supplemented by that of Doctor Anitra Karsten who has investigated the psychological and personality characteristics of older people.

---

*See p. 168, infra.

## Switzerland

In Basel, Doctor F. Verzár and his wife Jean have been conducting investigations on both the psychological and physiological aspects of aging at the Physiological Institute of the University of Basel. They have developed a large pet colony to provide them with aged animals for these studies. Doctor Verzár has investigated the differences in adaptation to environmental stresses such as high altitude and lowered temperature. His wife has conducted psychological studies to determine learning capacity at different age levels of the rat. Doctor Verzár in conjunction with several other investigators is conducting longitudinal studies of psychological and physiological changes in a group of relatively young employees of the Ciba Company in Basel.

## Netherlands

Doctor L. Van der Horst of the Psychiatric and Neurological Clinic of the Wilhelmina Hospital has studied the neurological and psychiatric aspects of aging. Doctor R. J. von Zonneveld has done a unique health study of all people over the age of 65, utilizing the services of practicing physicians all over the Netherlands.

## Canada

At McGill University, Doctor Dale Cameron has set up a gerontological unit which has been assessing the psychiatric and sociological adjustment of older people. At Montreal University, Hans Selye has applied his concepts of the general adaptation syndrome to the aging process.

### BIBLIOGRAPHY

1. Comfort, A.: *The Biology of Senescence.* New York, Rinehart, 1956.
2. Moise, J. E., Merritt, H. H., and Masselink, R. H. (eds.) : *The Neurological and Psychiatric Aspects of the Disorders of Aging,* Vol. 35. Res. Publ. Ass. Nerv. Ment. Dis., 1956, 307 pages.
3. Shock, Nathan: *Trends in Gerontology,* 2nd ed. Stanford, Calif., Stanford U. Press, 1957, pp. 173-185.

### General References

1. Jalavisto, Eeva: Adaptation of the phantom limb phenomenon as influenced by the age of amputees. *J. Gerontology, 5:*339-342, 1950.
2. Verzár, F.: *Lectures in Experimental Gerontology.* Springfield, Thomas, 1963.
3. Welford, A. T.: *Aging and Human Skill.* London, Oxford U. Press, 1958.

# Chapter VI

## SOCIAL AND CULTURAL FACTORS IN THE AGING PROCESS

THIS CHAPTER WILL BE DEVOTED to the impact of the aging process on the social structure and the social determinants of aging in the United States and a comparison of the aging process in cultures other than the American.

### AGING AND THE FAMILY

In the preindustrial society of craft and agrarian occupations, the family was a structure made up of at least three generations. In this family setting, it was possible for several generations to live together since the family structure was a productive unit. In the preindustrial society, old people were not only cared for but they also contributed to the subsistence and care of the family. Status was determined according to the productive patterns of individual members, and such factors as sympathy, love, and affection, which in recent times has been the basis of family life, were relatively insignificant compared to the family solidarity that was conditioned by function. Gradually, however, these functions were taken over by other institutions, primarily schools, clubs, etc., and in the work sector by mechanized machinery such as laundries, etc. Recreation, amusement, celebrations, and festivals now take place in business enterprises catering to these needs. Because of modern innovations, the family has been reduced to a unit of two and perhaps one and one-half generations. Insofar as the aged are concerned, the loss of some of the former tasks of the older people such as, for example, the instruction of the young, has weakened their bonds with the younger generation. The weakening of these bonds in the family structure has been enhanced by the replacement of education by the older generation (grandparents) by scientific or pseudoscientific education. The recommendations of modern psychology and education do not agree with the convictions of the older generation and there is subsequent complaint about the unappreciativeness of the older generation of such things as education of children, behavior of the marriage partner, life style, management of the household, etc. What is currently happening is that parents are fearful that the grandparents might take over the rearing of children and thus usurp their authority and parents are also fearful that education or attempts at rearing might compel the children to accept behavioral patterns and attitudes which might prevent the children from successfully adjusting to the contemporary expectations of society. Several other social and economic forces have contributed to the "setting apart" of the aged from the rest of the family and society. The first was the U. S. Supreme Court decision in the Inland Steel Case of 1949 which established pensions as a bargainable issue under the Taft-Hartley Act. This led to pension settlements in auto, steel, and other industries in which the company was to pay a maximum of $100 per month to the retired worker less the amount paid by Social Security. The revisions in Social Security legislation and the enactment of the Medicare Program has greatly improved the economic and health position of the aged, enabling their greater economic independence. What has happened is that increased mobility has created an extended-family modification, separate households for the generations, relative financial independence for each of the generations with bonds of voluntary assistance between them.

A word should be said here about the "family treatment model." Recently, students at the University of Michigan brought three generations of unrelated persons together for a weekend. All the participants found the experience very rewarding and one person organized an intergenerational commune. At Syracuse University a multigenerational dormitory has been operating, and has met with great success.

What is needed now is greater research concerning the interdependence of the generations. New terms are needed to adequately define the effects of the family structure on aging (e.g., a comparison of four generations vs. no relatives; loose emotional ties with relatives vs. none at all; and, being the head of a household vs. residing alone).

## Urban-Rural Changes

Changes in the rural-urban population are not yet completely understood by ecologists. The last 20 years has seen an apparent concentration of the urban aged in the older residential areas in the central sections of the large cities reflecting the urbanization and industrialization of society in general; the rural aged have migrated to the rural villages with the growth of retirement communities in Florida, California, and Arizona.

However, despite the predominant shift of the aged from rural to urban areas* the farm and rural centers of less than 3000 people still are "home" for many of the aged. Cowgill (3) analyzed the changes in the concentration of the aged in the central areas of 39 American cities and he discovered that although the percentage of aged in these areas continued to increase, this was due more to out-migration of the younger population than to the growth rate of the aged themselves. However, the apparent concentration of the aged in the central urban areas is a great sociological motivating force in the rise of various community services to the elderly. For example, the advent of such agencies as public housing, recreation, community centers, sheltered workshops, etc., has been shifted from children and young and middle-aged population to the aged with the concomitant birth of Golden Age Clubs and centers which specifically serve the needs of the elderly.

The development of retirement communities and villages in the milder climates in the United States, primarily inhabited by upper income groups of retired has created a new sociological development not only among the aged but also among the communities themselves. In some instances, there is duplication of

*See p. 12, supra.

surrounding facilities (in the town or village where the retirement village is located) and in others there is the requirement of additional facilities. This group (the retired in retirement villages) represents a pilot one for the study of the impact of leisure in our society.

## Social Class

Insofar as the aged are concerned, social class and cultural differences have a great impact on the health of the individuals. The aged who came from economically poor stock with a meager education lack a sufficient grasp of physiology and general health measures to take care of themselves. On the other hand, the middle and upper class aged because of greater reading and other public educational processes to which they are receptive and information readily available, do avoid adverse health events and reduce their consequences. Aged upper and lower class people live in different streams of information which influence their behavior, despite the efforts of the medical program to give simple information to the indigent sick aged. This is particularly true in the area of physical and mental health, so important to the aged. It is interesting to note that mortality rates, which are a criterion of environmental health, are twice as high in unskilled as professional aged workers. The difference is probably due to adverse conditions of work as well as related factors such as better nutrition and medical education which increased income bring.

At this point, it might be pertinent to comment on the aged who come from minority groups in the United States and one specifically which has had little attention, viz. the American Negro.

The social gerontological literature available on the Negro aged since 1950 is practically non-existant, and social gerontologists know almost nothing about the Negro aged. Most of the data on Negro aged pertains to their socio-economic conditions. In its study *Double Jeopardy, the Older Negro in America Today,* the National Urban League concluded that the Negro aged were in much poorer health than the white aged. On the other hand, Youmins found no significant differences between the subjective health ratings of Negro and white Kentucky subjects.

The 20th century has seen a dramatic increase in the number of aged Negroes in the United States. There has been a gain of 33 years in life expectation of the American Negro in the last 67 years. Lambing (Mary, L.)* in a doctoral dissertation at the University of Hawaii investigated the life style of American blacks who have retired from their professions, from stable blue collar workers, and from the service occupations, domestic work, and common labor. Data were collected through interviews with 33 men and 68 women ranging in ages from 48-105. The mean annual income was $1,244.40 for unmarried and $1,346.52 for married people. Although, more than half reported their income was insufficient to meet their needs, none were engaged in part time work. Some mentioned they were actively seeking work, but, were not successful because of their age. The professionals differed from the lower status groups in that they retired younger and had made voluntary decisions to leave work, rather than working until compulsory retirement age or being forced to quit because of poor health. This group also were more likely to make plans for their retirement years. Ownership of comfortable homes was characteristic of the professional group and most of the stable blue collar groups, whereas those of lower status more often paid rent and lived in poorer dwellings. The mean number of leisure time activities was 12.8 for the professionals, 6.3 for the stable blue collar workers and 4.1 for the unskilled group. Lambing concludes that many older Negroes in the lower classes have inadequate income, though they may have pensions of old age assistance.

The National Census on the Black Aged (NCBA), originating as an "ad hoc" interracial group was formed in November 1970 to further the cause of aged blacks. A special project of the NCBA known as the National Center on Black Aged was made possible by an Administration on Aging grant and opened in Washington, D.C. in October 1973. Its purpose is to provide a comprehensive

*The Gerontologist, volume 14 number 1, February, 1974 Lambing M.L., SOCIAL CLASS LIVING PATTERNS OF RETIRED NEGROES *The Gerontologist*, Part II, 12, 3, Autumn 1972 pp 285-288.

program to meet the needs of aged blacks, and is now the national clearinghouse on aged blacks.

Various studies show that the aged Negro derive their greatest source of satisfaction from religion as contrasted with his white counterpart where the greatest source of satisfaction is from family and relatives. In one study, Heymans and Jeffers (1) concluded that aged Negroes whose major lifetime occupations had been manual, attributed far more importance to religion than did non-manual aged Negroes.

Jackson (2) found that economic factors strongly affect affective involvement between aged Negro parents and their adult children. Those children and parents who seemed the most remote psychologically are also those who display the greatest economic need. Those parents who in their working years engaged in a manual occupation had great affection for their children and and visited their children more often when they received various goods and services from them. Most "non-manual" aged Negro parents were not economically dependent upon their adult children but are instead flowing aid from themselves to their children and grandchildren. However, most "manual" parents tend to feel that their children ought to assist in the provision of supplementary economic assistance, but do not rely upon them for sole assistance, placing greater dependency upon Social Security and welfare benefits. To what extent these conclusions about aged Negroes differ from those of aged whites will await the results of controlled studies.

Another minority group whose elderly have had little or no study are the older Chinese in the United States. In an article by Carp and Kataoka (Carp, Frances, and Kataoka, Eunice—Health Care Problems of the Elderly of San Francisco's Chinatown—The Gerontologist vol. 16, #1, Part I, February 1976, pp 30-38), the authors tell of the plight of the elderly Chinese in Chinatown in San Francisco. The information reported is selected from a larger study of 1.3% sample of San Franciscans aged 65 and older, which constituted 138 Chinese American residents of Chinatown. In addition to interviews, a set of 11 specially prepared apperception pictures was used to elicit stories; both an activity and food intake diary were recorded; each respondent described himself and was described by his interviewer through the use of an adjective check list.

62% of the respondents rated their health only as fair and 29% said it was poor. Twice as many (30%) Chinese as Caucasians (15%) elderly identified health as their most serious problem. Most of the Chinese elderly admitted to serious problems with mobility. Even in their own living quarters; 88% acknowledged trouble walking and negotiating stairs. In response to questions about specific health problems, Chinatown respondents reported 65% had trouble with slowness, 61% with moving, 48% with dizziness, 47% with vision and 52% with foot troubles, 43% usually went to a doctor once a month (probably most of these doctors did not hold medical degrees—for example herbalists are "doctors to the elderly Chinese American). Almost half of Chinatowns population subsits on income below the poverty level and the old tend to be among the poorest. 80% of the Chinese Americans who were interviewed live in households where yearly incomes were less than $4000 and 31% under $2000. The lives of the elderly Chinese are almost totally confined within Chinatown and they know nothing about the American health care system. Since few can converse in English, it was necessary to collect research data in Chinese. Because of the different dialects, the elderly Chinese cannot communicate symptoms to a Chinese doctor who does not speak the same dialect. These dialects which abound in the community separate Chinatown residents from each other and from the Chinese who only work there. There is a level of cost system and a network of social distinctions fostered by the influx of new immigrates vs the more established residents; and language and educational influences separate children and parents; thus the elderly Chinese in San Francisco's Chinatown are particularly prone to loneliness. One author of this article suggests a program to improve the well being of the elderly in Chinatown and should provide a place for them to gather and spend their days.

In a related article, Lurie, Kalish, Wexler, and Ansak (Lurie, Elinor; Kalish, Richard A; Wexler, Richard; and Ansak, Marie Louise, The Gerontologist, vol. 16 #1, Part I, February 1976 pp

39-46) at the ON LOK Senior Day Health Center which serves three principal groups in San Francisco, viz. Chinese, Filipino and Italian Americans in the Chinatown North Beach area of San Francisco, analyzed the ON LOK Senior Health Services provided primarily by a joint of the administration on aging. The ON LOK participants are predominately male (67%) and Chinese (73%), Filipinos (15%) and Italians (9%). Participants are primarily working class (65% were former unskilled or same-skilled workers) either widowed (43%), married (34%) and living alone in rented quarters or without a spouse only (21%). Over 90% here were born outside the United States, and although 2/3 have resided in this country 40 years or more, over 1/2 the entire group of participants are considered by the staff to speak little or no English. The average age is in the late 70's. 136 people participated in this study.

65% of this group require continuous medical supervision, 16% need supervision for one or more potentially life threatening conditions. Participants were also rated on their functional performance, i.e. the degree to which they could care for themselves and perform activities of daily living. Nearly half of the participants were evaluated as poor or considerably dependent; almost the same proportions were considered fair or somewhat dependent and 14% were seen as needing little or no help. Only 6% were judged fully capable of self care, and an additional 66% could care for themselves with some assistance from others.

In general concerning minorities, it seems that members of some minority groups may have specialized coping methods, e.g., different sets of standards and different ways of behaving normally than what we might call the "majority" groups. There are certain sociological factors that may strengthen minority groups. The "ghettoization" of minority groups may have strengthened internal ties among group members and relieved them from societal pressures; their relative low rate of institutionalization may be the result of cohesive family ties. Emotional strength among minorities may be interpreted from their low rates of neurotic disturbances and suicide. It has been shown that greater involvement in the mainstream of the common culture has increased the rate of institutionalization, suicide, and neurosis. Perhaps these trends could be averted by programs strengthening ethnic identities.

## Labor Force Participation

The economic factors and employment conditions of the aged have been discussed in pages 61-63. A further word should again be said about this important sociological aspect of aging.

Census data indicates that only 42% of white babies born in 1900 would survive up to the compulsory retirement age of 65. Today 75% will reach this age. Despite this, census data indicates that the *relative* number of aged *workers* have been shrinking consistently since 1900. The relative decline in this labor force is explainable on the basis of decreasing economic importance of agriculture due to a more industrialized society, mechanization and assembly line production in general, and self employment in the economy. With fewer farmers in the population and the increased organizational employment of professional people, the opportunity for staying gainfully employed for the aged has decreased. This is especially true because many people are retiring at an early age.

## Church and Political Participation

*Church Participation.* Studies of church attendance in the general population indicate that during the chronological age of the thirties there is a low point in religious observance, primarily, it is thought, because of the demands during that period of life, viz., occupational and career activity, homemaking, and the rearing of children. After the 30's, the trend is reversed, until people in their 60's reach a level of participation in religious and church activities equal to that of the teens. Recent studies show that there is a relationship between church membership and personal adjustment of the elderly, that is, the greater the church activity the better the adjustment. However, Moberg (3) showed that church membership as such is not so significant to adjustment in old age as many other studies have reported. One of the problems in the assessment of these variables is that many church members are members in name only and are concerned about church and its activities only on such occasions as Easter and Christmas, weddings and funerals, rather than a real devotion to religious beliefs. The essential criterion of activity is whether a true interest was developed and cultivated before the increased amount of leisure time allowed a higher rate of participation in church activities.

*Political Participation.* It can be predicted that by 1980 the balance of power in the U. S. electorate will be held by people over 60 which will inaugurate a new area of youth-age conflict. An interesting study by Kuhlen (4), shows that up to the age of 50, the proportion of men and women voting increases and then levels off until very late in life. In the area of local politics, interest in voting on local matters and in talking and reading about them increases until very late in life. However, participation in local activities like civic meetings and committee work increases until the late 40's and then decreases.

The role of the majority of older people in community and political affairs remains a real one. It may stem from the tendency on the part of our society to worry about what *to do* with the aged rather than what the aged generation *can do*. There is a growing tendency to see this segment of our population as one that needs protection rather than one which can help and protect itself. One of the means by which it can help itself is by greater participation in civic affairs which will overcome a kind of social stagnation replaced with civic competence, and it is hoped that 'a higher proportion of the aged generation can and will avail themselves of opportunities for participation in civic and political affairs. Evidence in several of the major voting behavior studies shows that the political influence of the aged may be much greater than population statistics show. A greater proportion of those people over 55 vote in presidential elections than do adults in any other age group, with the exception of the 45-55 group. However, it has been demonstrated that people over 55 rank last in "political efficacy."* This indicates despite the fact that older people do not have an optimistic view of their political effectiveness, they are determined nevertheless to participate politically. Various studies have shown that the popular conception

*The feeling that individual political action does or can have an impact on the political process.

that older people do not have an optimistic view of their own political economic panaceas is not necessarily true during "normal"
economic times. However, the experiences of the depression years
shows that if the country does not meet the social and economic
needs of the older segment of the population, the aged, like any
other social group, will develop political cohesiveness on the basis
of mutual insecurity.

In general, oldsters who identify themselves with one political
party the first time retain that affiliation with the party for which
they first cast a ballot. Likewise, people 55 and over tend to be
steadfast in their voting preference ranking the lowest in all age
groups as "split" voters and independents. Older people also are
more consistent in expressed pre-election intention and actual
voting preference than persons in other age groups. This should
be interpreted more as political consistency than inflexibility,
since sociological studies show that older people are receptive to
new ideas.

### Health

The subject of illness and physical health of the aged is a
complicated one and is not the subject of this text except as it
applies in a social context.

The prolongation of life in general has created new social
problems. The chronic progressive disorders of later life are becoming more prevalent and are creating the prospect of a medical survival for large numbers of aging people. This places a
tremendous burden on the health, nursing, domestic, and social
resources for all communities with consequent dependence on
governmental medical care. The Federal Medicare program and
the Medicaid programs of the states have arisen because of this
tremendous need.

Eisdorfer (Eisdorfer, Carl—Issues in Health Planning For The
Aged—The Gerontologist, vol. 16, #1, Part I, February 1976, pp
12-16) estimates that between the fiscal year 1960-1970, the annual
expenditures for health care in the U.S. increased from 24.4 billion
to approximately 69.5 billion dollars. The 1974 estimated expenditures are estimated at approximately 100 billion. Among the

various health care costs, the largest proportional growth from 1960-1970 was in the field of nursing home care. Nursing home costs now exceed 7 billion dollars annually and are growing steadily. According to the Department of Health, Education and Welfare about 80% of older Americans suffer from one or more chronic conditions, one of four older persons is hospitalized each year, and about 40% of the elderly have some condition which limits their activities of daily living; some 85% of the long-term care dollar is spent on older Americans.

The fact that more and more people in the population must live with, adapt to, and contend with the physiological signs of growing old such as impairment of the sensory and perceptual functions and degenerative chronic illness, makes it clear that in our current society, the aging person faces the possibility and almost the necessity of adjusting to the unavoidable risk of first submitting to prolonged physical disability and then succumbing to a degenerative disease. It is much more likely that now life will not end suddenly but come to an end in progressive internal decay. This will tax all the skills at the command of medical and behavioral scientists.

Various current Federal programs providing medical assistance have made what are now known as "nursing homes" the recipient of elderly patients. These institutions have come under close scrutiny in recent years because of the abuses of the patients in these homes, and various states are enacting legislation to correct such abuses.

In 1969, Gottesman and Bourestom did a study describing patient experience in nursing homes. The results indicate that nursing homes are increasing in size. In Michigan between 1950 and 1954 only 20% of the new homes licensed had over one hundred beds; between 1965 and 1969, forty-six were large homes. Mental hospitals have been moving towards centralized control, while nursing homes have been moving toward increased control by a few corporations. Mental hospitals have been trying to make more contacts with the non-institutionalized community, while nursing homes are becoming more cut off. Current legislation forces nursing homes to create distinctly separate parts with narrowly defined patient populations and rigid staffing patterns. Nursing homes must be skilled, intermediate, or basic care specialists or they cannot qualify for Federal monies that support eighty-seven percent of all nursing home patient's care. One of the big problems with nursing homes is that they are rewarded for keeping people sick. In a sense, nursing home patients are even less socially desirable than mental patients. Sixty-five percent of the patients in nursing homes stay in them over one year, and seventeen percent stay five years or more. The problem that mental hospitals have been trying to overcome, that of patients who have nothing to do for years at a time, is being replayed in nursing homes. Almost no nursing home patients make their own beds, cook, wash, iron, clean, shop, go for walks, or do anything else of potential "significance." Nursing homes are also caught in the vortex of public and private assistance. Most nursing homes developed as small, private enterprises, rather than as government or voluntary agencies. In the 1950's, with the advent of medicine legislation, the industry became controlled by people whose expertise was in business and construction. These people were not experienced in caring for aged people's psychological and medical needs, and now are dependent upon governmental financial support. This is an area of great friction and distrust between the government (who pays most of the bills) and the suppliers of nursing home services. An extenuation of the problem is that nursing homes are paid to meet goals that are unattainable. The fees are paid for curative and restorative services. However, the conditions that are primarily encountered are really not amenable to cure or rehabilitation.

An interesting concept, suggested by Matlack* and used for some time in Great Britain though not in the United States, is that of the geriatric day hospital. The pioneer for geriatric day hospitals was Doctor Lionel Z. Cosin, who found that the day hospital program, combined with a total commitment to maintaining the aged in the community, led to a significant reduction in beds occupied in nursing homes. Day hospitals are not the same as

---

*Matlack, David R., "The Case for Geriatric Day Hospitals," *The Gerontologist*, April, 15 (2): 109-113, 1975

senior centers. Day hospitals provide *remedial* services, while senior centers provide primarily mental and physical *stimulation* for their users. In the United States, the best facility for a geriatric day hospital would be geriatric in-patient services in the large community hospital; directed by the chief of the geriatric service of the parent hospital, and staffed by part-time physicians of the hospital, nurses, occupational therapists, psychologists, social workers, part-time speech therapists, podiatrists, and dentists.

**Sex Differences**

Excess male mortality over females is typical of almost all leading diseases, especially those of old age such as cardio-vascular disease and cancer. The only major chronic disease where the incidence is greater for women than men is diabetes.

It is estimated that currently there are 10 million widowed persons in the United States. Cleveland and Gianturco (Cleveland, Wm. P. and Gianturco, Daniel T., Remarriage Probability After Widowhood: A Retrospective Method—Journal of Gerontology, 1, 31, January 1976, pp 99-103) devised a technique to estimate remarriage probabilities with respect to age for newly widowed persons utilizing North Carolina marriage certificates plus information from the 1970 U.S. Census. Remarriage probabilities are very high for persons widowed before the age of 35. White men have the highest remarriage probabilities. Approximately 90% of younger white widowers remarry. Over half of the white widowed men, between 46 and 65 remarry. Substantial numbers continue to remarry even beyond the age of 65. White women have a higher probability of remarriage below age 35. Beyond 35 the probability of remarriage decreases sharply and is considerably lower than their male counterparts. There is a similar sex difference for blacks. Remarriage probabilities for both groups (male & female) are lower than for their white counterparts.

Less than 1/4 of men widowed after age 65 ever remarry. Less than 5% of women widowed after age 55 ever remarry. Men remarry more quickly than women, the medium interval to remarriage 1.7 years for men and 3.5 years for women.

An interesting study is reported by Atchley (Atchley, Robert C. Journal of Gerontology 31, 2, March 1976, pp 204-211) where data was gathered by questionnaires mailed to a random sample of retired teachers in a large midwestern state and to the entire population of people retired from a midwestern telephone company in order to measure sex differences on certain variables which were;

1. Importance of work.
2. Attitude toward retirement.
3. Time required to become accustomed to retirement.
4. Loneliness.
5. Anxiety.
6. Anomie (ability to adjust to change).
7. Age identification (self description as very old, old, just past middle age, and middle aged).
8. Self esteem, stability of self concept and sensitivity to criticism.
9. Depression.
10. Self reported health.
11. Income adequacy.
12. Perceived contact with friends.
13. Participation in organizations.

In general the results show that compared to older men, older women were found to be as work-oriented and more likely to take a long time adjusting to retirement. Older women were more likely to report "negative" psychological symptoms while older men were more likely to see changes in social participation. Based on the findings of this study, men respond to aging in terms of how it affects their relations to the social system. Among the semi-skilled and unskilled groups, aging seems to bring about a desirable disengagement. As compared to middle class men, they less often remain in the labor force and are less involved with friends and organizations compared with the past. This particular sample of working class men had reasonably good health and adequate income.

Compared with older men, older women are less likely to respond to aging in active terms such as staying in the labor force or increasing social participation, and more often deny they are old. However; older women are more likely to be lonely, anxious and depressed, have low self esteem and be highly sensitive to criticism. Women respond in general to aging with higher levels of social stress.

In a study by Jaslow (Jaslow, Phillip, Employment, Retirement and Morale Among Older Women, Journal of Gerontology, 31, 2, March 1976, pp 212-218) he attempted to apply to females the role theoretical orientation to work and retirement to women in old age which has often applied to men. The object of the study was to test the hypothesis that older working women have better morale than those who do not work. 2398 women with a mean age of 72.9 years were asked about the following variables:

1. Income.
2. Morale—using a morale scale using the Lawtin Morale Scale.
3. General Health.
4. Physical incapacity.
5. Employment status.

With the exception of women with annual incomes over $5,000, the findings show a statistical difference both between older working women (who had the best morale) and retirees, and between retirees as never having worked, the latter group evidenced the lowest morale. The results also indicate that work has a salutary psychological influence among women past 65 years.

## Urbanization, Disease and Mortality

The Western states of the U. S. have the lowest mortality rate with the rural West, North Central Division the best of this division. The industrial and urban Northeast and middle Atlantic States have the highest mortality rate. The South also has a high mortality rate but not quite as high as the Northeast and Middle Atlantic States. In general, the kind of accessible health resources and the hazards of the environment in metropolitan areas are more important than rural-urban contrasts. It is interesting to note that the higher the degree of urbanization of a given area, the wider is the mortality differential between the sexes. A survey of male-female mortality within metropolitan areas in New

York State shows that excess male mortaility varied from 39% in cities with populations of 50,000 and over to about 29% in towns under 10,000 (5).

Social and ocupational class membership are also associated with male-female mortality differential. Studies of mortality patterns indicate a noticeable downward trend in mortality among men as their socio-economic level declines while the reverse pattern seems to apply to women.

### Aging in Countries Other than the U.S.

An examination of the age structure of foreign countries shows a variation in the persons 65 and over varying from a minimum of 1.5% in Togoland and the Gold Coast to a maximum of 11.8% in France. Defining as relatively aged those countries with 7% or more of their population in the age group 65 and over, there are 19 countries in this category comprising about 1/5 of the world's population.

TABLE 11

PERCENTAGE DISTRIBUTIONS OF PEOPLE 65 AND OVER
IN SELECTED POPULATIONS

| Country | Per cent 65 & over |
|---|---|
| *AFRICA* | |
| Algeria (Moslems) | 2.70 |
| Angola | 2.93 |
| Basutoland (Africans) | 6.24 |
| Egypt | 3.10 |
| Gold Coast | 1.52 |
| Mozambique | 2.24 |
| Togoland (UK) | 1.46 |
| Union of South Africa | |
| Europeans | 6.18 |
| Non-Europeans | 3.64 |
| *NORTH.AMERICA* | |
| Alaska | 3.69 |
| Canada | 7.75 |
| Costa Rica | 2.89 |
| Cuba | 3.34 |
| Dominican Republic | 2.86 |
| El Salvador | 2.96 |
| Greenland | 2.17 |
| Guatemala | 2.61 |
| Haiti | 4.00 |
| Honduras· | 3.97 |
| Jamaica | 3.92 |
| Mexico | 3.36 |
| Nicaragua | 2.85 |
| Puerto Rico | 3.80 |
| Trinidad and Tobago | 4.11 |

TABLE 11 — PERCENTAGE DISTRIBUTIONS OF PEOPLE 65 AND OVER
IN SELECTED POPULATIONS (Continued)

| Country | Per cent 65 & over |
|---|---|
| USA | 8.18 |
| *SOUTH.AMERICA* | |
| Argentina | 3.92 |
| Brazil | 2.45 |
| British Guiana | 3.99 |
| Chile | 3.50 |
| Colombia | 2.90 |
| Ecuador | 3.54 |
| Panama | 3.23 |
| Paraguay | 3.72 |
| Peru | 4.32 |
| Venezuela | 2.66 |
| *ASIA* | |
| Burma | 2.83 |
| Ceylon | 3.48 |
| Formosa | 2.50 |
| India | 3.58 |
| Israel | 4.00 |
| Japan | 4.94 |
| Jordan | — |
| South Korea | 3.70 |
| Malaya | 3.21 |
| Philippines | 3.15 |
| Thailand | 2.58 |
| Turkey | 3.41 |
| *EUROPE* | |
| Austria | 10.13 |
| Belgium | 11.05 |
| Czechoslovakia | 7.58 |
| Denmark | 9.11 |
| Finland | 6.62 |
| France | 11.79 |
| Germany: Federal Republic | 9.28 |
| Germany: USSR Zone | 9.98 |
| Great Britain | 10.83 |
| Greece | 6.31 |
| Hungary | 6.97 |
| Iceland | 7.52 |
| Ireland | 10.69 |
| Italy | 8.06 |
| Netherlands | 7.86 |
| Norway | 9.64 |
| Poland | 5.08 |
| Portugal | 6.98 |
| Spain | 7.23 |
| Sweden | 10.32 |
| Switzerland | 9.57 |
| Yugoslavia | 5.67 |
| *OCEANIA* | |
| Australia | 8.02 |
| New Zealand (excl. Maoris) | 9.58 |
| New Zealand (Maoris) | 2.54 |
| USSR | 4.10 |

Source: United Nations, Demographic Yearbooks.

All of these are identified with Western culture, and comprise only a small proportion of the world population. There is no known data on the Soviet Union. The results of the various local censuses undertaken in -1940 and the following years make it virtually certain that the Chinese population belongs to the least aged category. There are reasons to believe that the percentage of the aged (over 65) in the Soviet Union is at present 6-8%. At the beginning of the present century, some populations were considered aged—this is so in Sweden, France, and Norway, where the percentage of old people are 8.47, 8.2, and 7.9, while on the other hand the population of Great Britain and of Germany which today belongs to the most aged populations had less than 5% of old people in 1900. Thus, the growth of the aged population in the remaining European countries is a relatively recent phenomenon.

## CARE OF THE AGED IN FOREIGN COUNTRIES

### Europe

Although the care and interest in the aged in other countries is not as extensive as that in the United States, the United States can learn a good deal from the experience of foreign countries. In general, the physical care of the aged in Europe can be placed into two main categories:

1) Villages — Usually composed of a number of different types of villages and living arrangements with some communal facilities, and centralized services.
2) Proximate Housing — those providing some services in addition to maintenance and those offering maintenance only.

Most of the housing projects in Europe are for the most part aggregates of various types of accommodations designed to serve the needs of old people with various degrees of frailties and illnesses. They supply protective oversight, medical service, and nursing care, communal dining rooms, housekeeping services, and planned recreational, social, occupational activities, and religious programs.

**Scandinavian Countries**

Old People's Town in Copenhagen, Denmark is the best known of the European Villages for older people. It has been in operation since 1919 and has been under the enlightened medical direction of Dr. Torbin Geill. It offers accommodations for 1600 persons or about $3\frac{1}{2}\%$ of Copenhagen's old age pensioners. It was built at the cost of 2 million dollars ($12\frac{1}{2}$ million Kroners) with an annual operating expenditure of about $6\frac{1}{2}$ million Kroner ($900,000). Each person pays for his accommodations from his pension although allowed a monthly allowance of 26 Kroner, $4 per day. The general section of the village has 9 large residence halls which house approximately $\frac{1}{2}$ the population. New buildings have been erected which are four stories high and are equipped with elevators. On each floor is a kitchenette and small sitting room for visiting, reading, and listening to the radio. Each building has accommodations for bathing. The resident rooms contain an ante-room for a wardrobe and lavatory and are connected with a nurses' station by a buzzer system. There is a hospital caring for both the chronically and acutely ill. In addition, there is a space assigned to labs, x-ray, physical therapy, therapeutic baths and other types of equipment as well as research facilities.

In addition to the hospitals and residence halls, villages include an auditorium, church, morgue, service buildings (kitchen, heating plant) housing for personnel and an administration building. The village operates under the general supervision of the Social Welfare Department of the Municipality of Copenhagen. The staff of the village contains a governor who has general administrative responsibility and chief medical officer who has charge of hospitals and medical care-program. Other staff include physicians, physiotherapists, occupational therapists, social workers, nurses, orderlies, and maintenance workers. The average age of the pensioners is 76 for men and 78 for women. No work is expected of them but they can volunteer for light work in the garden or kitchens and receive a small payment in return. About 10% of the residents work. There are movies, concerts, theatrical performances, and a library containing 8000 volumes. Occupational therapy is available in both the hospital and general section.

In Sweden, there is not much provision for the segregation of older people. The exception is Sabaatsberg located in the central part of the city of Stockholm. The accommodations are for:

1) A Nursing Home. This functions as a modern geriatric hospital for 370 chronically sick or disabled patients.
2) An intermediary type of dwelling which houses 75 persons in need of personal care who do not need the medical resources of the hospital nursing home.
3) Home for the Aged. Here are housed several hundred pensioners who are well enough to look after themselves but who for social reasons cannot be accommodated in the community.

Strong emphasis is placed upon physical restoration and activity programs. Occupational therapy is encouraged because the staff has found that it keeps up morale, reduces the amount of nursing care required, lessens personality disturbances, promotes better eating habits, and retards or prevents onset of weakness and debilitation which comes when old people are idle or kept in bed. In addition to the occupational therapy program, the other activities offered include parties, trips to town, crafts, classes in foreign languages, visits to relatives, and holidays away from the institution. On the staff are the Chief Medical Officer, two full time staff doctors, two physical therapists, one occupational therapist, and an assistant, and a battery of nurses.

Trevenkhie-Sovietetaan in Helsinki, Finland, is a kind of rehabilitation hospital which emphasizes restoration and rehabilitation of patients and provision of a comfortable home for them.

## England

Whiteley Village in Whiteley Park near London is a quiet community with well kept lawns where the occupants can be seen tending flowers and vegetables. There is a hospital for chronically ill or acutely ill patients. The village contains twice as many women as men.

## Other Countries in Europe

Riehler-Heimstatten, in Cologne, Germany, is very similar to Old People's Town in Copenhagen. Not much attention is paid to rehabilitation but the emphasis is more on custodial care.

A rather interesting experimental home is in Agafton, Rumania, a village in the Suceava region. The home is inside a local village and residents maintain permanent relations with the local population of every age. The settlement spreads over 54 acres consisting mostly of orchards but also contains a vineyard where crops are grown. Fruit trees, a vegetable garden, flowers, cultivated by senior residents surround each cottage. The residents raise food, rabbits, and bees. The medical unit is supervised by a physician who grants regular and permanent medical assistance. Medicine is distributed free of charge. Emphasis is placed on occupational therapy. The nature of the work and amount of physical effort is determined by the health, past activities, aptitudes, and personal wishes of the indivduals. According to their individual interests, the residents can listen to the radio, attend movies and lectures, and participate in discussion on various subjects.

Because of the large number of pensioners in Europe, segregation into large housing developments have been rejected in favor of building blocks of pensioners' flats or apartments as part of regular housing developments and distributing pensioners' flats throughout ordinary apartment houses. Studies made in England showed that if suitable housing is available, families will tend to concentrate in a given district. Thus, they may be near one another but not live under the same roof. Under these circumstances families can render reciprocal services during illness and old age. In Holland, old age homes are reserved for those people in need of daily nursing service and independent dwellings are provided for those still able to manage their own households.

The Old Age Assistance Act ensures adequate resources for all old people, correlated to the help their children can provide. A pension payable at age 65 is based on the national wage index. The current (1976) pension rates are: single persons, 651.50 guilders per month; and, married couples, 909 guilders per month. In 1968, about two-thirds of the total work force of 3.9 million were working toward a second pension. The elderly sick in Holland are cared for in institutions called nursing homes ("Verpleegtehuizen"—not exactly the same as nursing homes in the U.S.), which are fully paid by the state. In recent years, these have been increasing attention on care for the mentally disturbed; much of this pioneering work has been done at Nieuw Toutenburg, a home for the elderly mentally disturbed in Friesland.

To encourage the building of independent living quarters for pensioners, national legislation has been enacted by a number of countries to provide building subsidies to municipalities for pensioners' dwellings built as regular parts of housing programs. Subsidies have also been made available to private associations and church groups, this materially increasing the total amount of housing provided for older people. Not nearly enough housing, however, has as yet been provided. Independent housing has taken various forms. In England there are many row housing projects and in Holland detached buildings of one or two stories are often built adjacent to the new 3 or 4 story worker apartment buildings. In Denmark, Sweden, Switzerland, and West Germany, the pensioners' housing seems most frequently to be in the form of 2-3 story buildings each containing a number of flats or apartments. In order to qualify for a subsidy, the dwellings must usually be equipped to make it easier for elderly people to manage housework on their own. As a rule, a manager is in charge who oversees maintenance of buildings and assists residents by making arrangements in times of crises. In some instances, a matron is also responsible for planning recreational and other types of group work. Activity facilities are limited to assembly halls, lounges, libraries, and occasionally craft shops. Provisions are also made for outdoor diversions such as gardening, croquet, and bowling on the green. There is also a tendency to separate able-bodied from the frail and the sick.

For several years, a group of social scientists from different countries have been making comparative cultural studies of adjustment to retirement in their respective countries. Included are the countries of Austria, France, England, West Germany, the Netherlands, Italy, Poland, and the United States. The study, consisted initially of a sample of retired male school teachers, aged 70-75, in each of the countries, they were studied and the people in their social universe examined. The following items were assessed: present level of activity, degree of satisfaction regarding present level of activity, extent of ego involvement with the people in his social universe, or change of activity level since the age of 60, and his affect concerning the change of role activity. This is done by means of rating scales. The final purpose of this study is to ascertain how the social settings affect the process of adjustment in later life in different cultures and countries. The tentative pilot findings were reported at the International Congress of Gerontology at Vienna in 1965.*

More definitive welfare data are available for certain countries in Europe.

### England

The total number of people over 65 in Great Britain has risen from 6.8% in 1915 to 16% in 1975. In 1959 the population over 80 was 1.8%, in 1974 it was 2.25% and projections indicate it will be 2.88% in 1980.

In Great Britain under the British Social Security System, insured persons retiring from regular employment qualify for a retirement pension at any time after reaching the age of 65 and 60 for women. Men, on reaching the age of 65, are considered as retired whether or not they are still working. Pensions are increased for people who are working between the ages of 65 and 70, that is a bonus given for people working between the ages of 65 and 70. Practically every profession or trade has its special ways for pensions and allowances for its aged members from the Royal Benevolent Medical Fund who care for aged members of the medical profession and dependents to the Ice Cream Vendor's Benevolent Fund having similar provisions for its members. In England, there are provisions according to the National Assistance Act whereby local authorities provide residential homes for the

*For further information in regard to this study, it is suggested that the reader contact: Professor Robert J. Havighurst, Committee on Human Development, University of Chicago, Chicago, Illinois 60637.

aged and the National Health Service with its three main components—the hospital service, a local health authority service for preventative work, and to help those who are sick at home and a general practitioner service enabling all to have a family doctor. The British government is currently trying to integrate these services so that all elderly people may be accommodated.

There are about 7½ million (15% of the total population) people of pensionable age in Great Britain today. Half a million are known to be employed full or part time. At the present time, the Britsh government is trying to add and strengthen those services which enable the elderly to remain in their own homes and special housing for the elderly.

The number of elderly living alone has doubled in the last ten years to nearly twenty-five percent of all elderly. Flat rate national insurance retirement pensions are ten pounds a week for single persons and sixteen pounds for married.

The National Assistance Act gives financial aid to voluntary associations whose activities provide recreation for the elderly. There are about 350 such clubs and 50 all day centers functioning today.

Developing welfare services for all classes of handicapped persons under the National Assistance Act has provided increasing care for the elderly who are also handicapped. Until 1960, it was only the blind that were taken care of, but currently this has been extended to all handicapped persons. A study in 1968 showed that home help service for the elderly needed to be doubled.

## Switzerland

Switzerland has a Federal Old Age and Survivor's Insurance Act enacted in 1948 whereby Swiss workers contribute to the fund from their wages on a graduated scale according to income. However, full annuities are not due until 1968. The Swiss Foundation Pro Senectute, a private organization, is the only organization in Switzerland which exclusively cares for old people. It relies mainly on the results of public collections, donations, and legacies as well as subsidies of the cantons and municipalities. It pays annuities to people over 65. An interesting element of this Foundation is that it pays annuities to *foreigners* living in Switzerland. Other activities of this Foundation are a social one, providing recreation for the older citizens of Switzerland and providing jobs for healthy older people who are willing to work.

## Luxembourg

The progress being made in Europe can be illustrated by the enactment of old age assistance in the tiny Grand Duchy of Luxembourg. In 1960, the National Solidarity Fund Bill was passed which guarantees a minimum income to older handicapped people by payment of pensions to qualified persons. There are also senior citizens homes. The Maison de Geriatue et de Retraite is a pilot institution for both well and sick older persons located at Hamm, a suburb of the city of Luxembourg, for the purpose of studying the problem of caring for the aged.

## South America

The problem of the aged in South America is not as acute as that in other countries since only about 10% of the people live to be over 60 years of age. In most Latin American countries (with the exception of Mexico), there is no special housing for older people. An example of the kinds of assistance given to older people is that of Chile where men over 65 and women over 60 are entitled to a pension calculated according to the amount of their contribution during their working years. In addition, full medical care is provided in the hospitals and out patient clinics as well as home care by doctors, nurses, and social workers.

## Canada

In Canada, old age security is paid to everyone in the country over 70 by the Federal Government and the most received is $40 per month. Each of the provinces also has a scheme for old age assistance for people from 65-70. The government as a whole does little planning for the needs of older people. One of the interesting elements of the Canadian problem is that in some parts of Canada there are practically no old people while in others there is an undue proportion. Where there is an undue proportion, there are long lists of old people requiring residential care. In Canada, there is no national organization devoted to the welfare of older people.

**Israel**

Israel is a relatively young country and there are about 5% of people in that new country over the age of 65 (Jews 5.8%, Moslems 3.8%, Christians 5.2%, and Druses 4.3%). However, the persons in the age bracket of 65 and over is increasing continuously and the forecast is that 8% of the population will be over 65 in the next 7 years. According to law, every resident is insured under the National Insurance Scheme and will receive a pension after the age of 65. After the initial provision of the establishment of institutional care for the aged there is a trend toward accepting the philosophy that the place of the aged is near his family, relatives and friends. There are several collective housing projects with house help service, housing units near homes for the aged, two occupational centers, a goodly number of recreational clubs, apartments for the aged, and a few sheltered workshops.

There are also "homes for the aged"* with bed capacities of 150-100, an old people's village with more than 1000 beds. Almost 80% of the population is enrolled in insurance plans mainly in the Sick Fund Organization of the Labor Union, which provides free access to a network of clinics throughout the country.

One of the large agencies which takes care of the aged is the American Joint Distribution Committee (A.J.D.C.) called the Mulben Joint. Its responsibilities are the care of aged new immigrants. The Labor Union Agency for the Aged** is another organization of healthy aged members of the Union which has instituted 600 beds in newly built institutions, housing projects for 300 persons with 260 apartments close to homes for the aged, and seven clubs with 3500 members.

Every third man over 65 and every fifth person of this age of both sexes is employed and more than one-half of all people over 65 work part time. In 1965, a special organization known as Homeshakem (Rehabilitator) was established. This agency, affiliated with the Ministry of Labor, employs aged five hours daily as clerical workers, janitors and gardeners, watchmen, and sundry

---

*Called Bater Avot (Parents Homes).

**Called Mishon.

jobs in small workshops. A voluntary agency called Lefe-Lene for the aged maintains four special workshops for the aged where people work three hours daily.

Interesting programs are being carried out in Israel from which people in the United States can profiit. Israel, like the United States, has an immigrant population, but of very recent origin. The immigrants consist essentially of three distinct groups. Of Israel's present day population of two million, 7% are over the age of 60 but of these only 45 are over the age of 65; within the total aged population, 58%, come from Western countries, 38% from Asia and Africa, and 4% are native born. Thus there are 3 different segments of the aged immigrant Israeli society:

1) The group of Israelis from technically and economically developed countries with a Western oriented way of life.
2) The groups from various Oriental countries (Middle East) — Africa (Morocco, Algiers, Tunisia, Egypt) — Asia (Yemen and Iraq) with strong family, cultural, and religious traditions of their own, different from the ways of life of Israel. These people have discarded some of their old ways of life but are having problems adapting to the new world in Israel.
3) Other people of Oriental background who have steadfastly maintained their old cultural background and preserved their tradition. This group is composed primarily of Yemenite Jews.

*Group I.* The Association of Aged Persons in Jerusalem was founded by a group of aged European immigrants most of whom live with their children, to provide social and cultural needs. Activities assumed the form of lectures and discussion groups on various subjects including the problem of growing old. Volunteers from the Association (who are often retired themselves) work with people in old age homes who suffer from loneliness and isolation and they are taken to concerts and meetings. An organization known as Organization for Immigrants from Central Europe* has opened up boarding houses for aged persons with

---

*In Israel, such organizations are known as Landsmannschaften which are organizations formed by people from a common country of origin for the purpose of

the same cultural heritage.

*Group II.* Most of the aged of this group belong to the lower socio-economic structure of the country. In Jerusalem, an example of the kind of work that is being done with this Oriental group is in a particular neighborhood in Jerusalem whose residents are almost all North African immigrants. The municipal social services have set up community centers for these aged immigrants and trained group leaders of the same cultural background to work with this aged immigrant group, to help them adjust to the new situation. Group excursions are held twice a year to bring the aged closer to the life of the new country. Part-time employment is also provided for these people to relieve some of the oppressive economic conditions of these elderly people.

*Group III.* This group has remained almost unaltered and change in their social values is very slow. The patriarchal traditions of religious and social life in the extended family unit have continued on, so that there is no need to alter this. The older men participate in the meetings of the homes of their leaders where the problems of the community are discussed. Prayer and religious study take up much of the time of the aged and there does not seem to be a need for organized governmental and private intervention.

The United States still has strongly entrenched aged immigrant groups some of whom cling to their old world values and who present a problem to their children and society. In looking to the experiments on immigrants in Israel, we can learn much which may assist us in handling such immigrant groups in the United States.

## Japan

Over 75% of all Japanese aged 65 or more live with their children. (Office of the Prime Minister 1973). The majority of Japanese men over 65 continue to be in the labor force (Japan Census Bureau 1965). Japanese older persons are not only permit-

furthering their integration by meeting jointly to foster their specific economic, and cultural needs.

ted, but expected to continue working at some kind of job as long as they are able.

Most of the older Japanese who are not employed continue to be useful in housekeeping, child care, shopping, and gardening. The vast majority of Japanese older people also remain active in their committees through government supported Elders Club—Analagous to Senior Citizens Clubs in the United States. A program to improve the health of Japanese elders is a free annual health examination and treatment for those that need it. In 1973, the Japanese government began providing completely free medical care to most Japanese over the age of 70. Some cities provide free medical care to their residents between the ages of 65-70

With the relatively recent democratization and influence of the United States, a great deal of progress has been made in the geriatric field. In 1963, the Law for the Welfare of the Aged was drawn up by the National Government which enhanced the physical and mental health of the aged in Japan and also provided work for older people. One of the unique provisions of this law is the enhancement of prestige of older persons who made contributions to society in the past. A Central and Local Council of Social Welfare has also been set up by the government to encourage social and recreational events for the aged. Old People's Clubs have mushroomed throughout the country. In 1962, the National Association of Old People's Clubs was established and has grown to about three million members. The national government has also instituted an "Old People's Day" in 1951* at which time the contributions of the elderly are recognized and extolled, and celebration of that day has grown to a national festival.

There have been new efforts in helping the aging in Japan. In April 1973 a Special Permanent Standing Committee on Aging cleared by the prime minister was formed. The Committee consists of representatives from all the Ministries with programs related to the elderly. Presently the overall quality and thesis of planning for the elderly in Japan is one of seeking advice by the

---

*September 15 is the day.

council of the aged themselves in a particular program, local offerings, local and national welfare advisory councils and public opinion shaped by the mass media.

## Chinese

Traditionally the Chinese venerated old age, and the elders had the unqualified respect of the juniors. The circumstances surrounding the Chinese aged can be gathered from a study by Ikels in Hong Kong, a city which is ninety-eight percent Chinese. According to data provided by the Census and Statistics Department on the Future Needs of the Elderly, thirty-one percent of people over the age of sixty were still gainfully employed in 1971. At present, there is no contributory social security system in Hong Kong nor are there employer-sponsored pension schemes (also true in Taiwan)*, except in the case of government employees. Medical treatment for the elderly is practically free, but this is no different from other age groups in Hong Kong for government subsidized services. There are private hospitals, some of which charge fees which put them well beyond the reach of the majority of the population. As of 1973, there were twenty-one "homes" for the aged; most of which are supported by religious organizations. This is the situation which also essentially exists in Taiwan.

## The Soviet Union

In very recent years, we have gathered a great deal of information on the treatment of older people in the Soviet Union.

There seems to be a genuine respect, special favor, and treatment of older people in Russia. The love and respect that older people enjoy in a peasant society seems to have diffused into the people of the Soviet Union. Older people live with their children and are encouraged to lead active and useful lives. All older people are called "grandmother" or "grandfather" and they are helped in such areas as seats on public transportation, they do not stand in line and do not carry heavy packages. One half of the older people in Russia live in rural villages and are able to en-

*There is no data on this in the People's Republic of China.

gage in agricultural work at least part of the year. They may work for wages during the busy planting season or at harvest time. Elderly people seldom live alone and most older people move in with their children when they cannot manage themselves. Although there are government homes for the aged, none of the homes are filled to capacity because most move in with their children. The older people who live on farms are integrated into the life of the community; this is also true in the cities.

The retirement age for men is 60 and women is 55—low according to Western standards. However, this is not compulsory and many people remain at work many years after they are eligible to retire. The pensioner receives at least one half of his former income, and it is possible to have a pension that is practically the same as his working wage.

Money of the pensioner in Russia goes further than the person on a pension in the United States primarily because the basic items for pensioners in Russia are either free or very reasonable. Medical bills are paid by the State. Comforts and luxuries in the U.S.S.R. are not as available as in the U. S. to the *entire* population so that retirement even on a reduced pension does not bring about a marked decrease in living conditions. The added hours of free time enable retired people to enjoy movies, lectures, drama, and other special attractions which are free; older people receive special rates at museums, athletic events, and theatres.

Since physical health is an important aspect of life for the aged in Russia as well as in other countries, two special kinds of health institutions have been set up by the government. The first is the system of health resorts called Kurorts which are open to people of all ages and where the patient stays for about a month and is given exhaustive health exams to determine the kind of treatment that is most effective. Various kinds of treatments have been instituted much of it in the area of "natural" therapy (mineral water, sun bathing, physical exercise, etc.). The Social Security Administration pays expenses if the person is retired.

The second innovation is that of establishment by the government of "Zones of Health" which can be attended by people of all ages, but are primarily attended by older people. These are located in the cities, and resemble outpatient clinics in which the older person lives at home but visits the center several times a week for treatment. Most of the older people at the Zone of Health take part in a physical culture program consisting of early morning exercises such as setting up exercises, self massage, and rhythm exercises. The entire program consists of swimming, hiking, boating, drinking mineral water, baths, etc. In addition to meeting the health requirements of older people, the Zones of Health serve as a center for socialization.

Although life expectancy in the Soviet Union is similar to that in the United States, the survival rate at age 70 and 80 is higher in the United States, but the survival rates at age 90 and 100 are much higher in the Soviet Union. Although the United States has more people who are 80 years of age and over, the U.S.S.R. has twice as many who are 100 and older. Thus, there is the strange situation in comparing the two countries insofar as longevity is concerned, that fewer people live to be old in the U.S.S.R. but more people who do attain old age live to be older. The reason may be because of the extended health services to older people in the U.S.S.R.

## BIBLIOGRAPHY

1. Heymans, D., and Jeffers, F.: Study of the relative influence of race and socio-economic status upon the activities and attitudes of a southern aged population. *J. Gerontology, 19:*225-229, 1964.
2. Jackson, Jacqueline J.: Elderly Parents: Their Affective Relationship with Their Adult Children. Paper Read at American Psychological Assn. Meeting, Washington, D. C., Sept. 1967.
3. Moberg, D. O.: Church membership and personal adjustment in old age. *J. Gerontology, 8:*207-211, 1953.
4. Kuhlen, R. G.: Extension and Constriction of Life Activities During the Adult Life Span. Unpublished Ms. Read at the Second International Gerontological Congress, St. Louis, Missouri, 1951.
5. Parkhurst, E.: Differential mortality in New York State Exclusive of New York City, by age, sex and cause of death according to degree of urbanization. *Am. J. Public Health, 46:*959-965, 1956.
6. Lambing, M.L.: Social Class Living Patterns of Retired Negroes. *The Gerontologist,* Part II, *12:*3, 285-288, Autumn 1976.
7. Carp, F. and Kataoka, E.: Health Care Problems of the Elderly of San Francisco Chinatown. *The Gerontologist,* Part I, *16:*1, 30-38, February, 1976.

8.   Atchley, R.C.: Selected Social and Psychological Differences Between Men and Women in Later Life. *Journal of Gerontology, 31:2*, 204-211, March, 1976.
9.   Jaslow, P.: Employment, Retirement and Morale Among Older Women. *Journal of Gerontology, 31:2*, 204-211, March, 1976.
10.  Eisdorfer, C.: Issues in Health Planning for the Aged. *The Gerontologist,* Part I, *16:1*, 12-16, February, 1976.

## General References

1. Tibbets, C. (ed.): *Handbook of Social Gerontology.* Chicago, Univ. of Chicago Press, 1960, pp. 208-260.

# INDEX

183